ASAN
AUTISTIC SELF ADVOCACY NETWORK

Empowering

Leadership

A Systems Change Guide for
Autistic College Students
and Those with Other Disabilities

A Collaborative Project Funded by

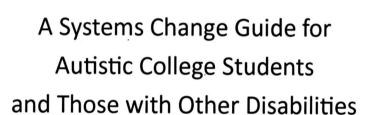

THE DANIEL JORDAN
FIDDLE
FOUNDATION.
FOR ADULT AUTISM
DEVELOPING | ADVOCATING | FUNDING

First Edition July 2013
ISBN-13: 978-1-938800-04-7
Library of Congress Cataloging-in-Publication Data has been applied for.

Table of Contents

We give special thanks and gratitude to all of our contributors.

Linda Walder Fiddle
Ari Ne'eman
Allegra Stout
Elizabeth Boresow
Alex Umstead
Melanie Yergeau
Alec Frazier
Leah Jane Grantham
Emily Kronenberger
Mike Liu
Cara Liebowitz
Steven Kapp

Foreword

By Linda Walder Fiddle
Founder and Executive Director
The Daniel Jordan Fiddle Foundation

The Daniel Jordan Fiddle Foundation is excited to have funded and collaborated with the Autistic Self Advocacy Network on this cutting-edge project that is aimed to enhance the higher education experiences, and life beyond the university, for the diverse population of individuals on the autism spectrum and also for individuals who have other disabilities. The hallmark of our organization has been to open doors for people to live fulfilling and productive lives, and we believe that there should be no limitations to the possibilities for individuals living with disabilities to achieve their personal goals and attain the dreams they have for themselves.

The opportunity to attend a college or university program provides individuals with a pathway for achieving these goals and it is our hope that this booklet enables them to more successfully navigate it. In addition, it is our hope that this booklet becomes a resource for school administrators and the general school population and also for all individuals living with a disability as they participate in and contribute to community life.

We hope that everyone who encounters this resource will find the information and advocacy ideas presented helpful in advancing their own educational and life experiences. The chapters of this booklet can be used as a starting point and guidepost that inspires and supports your journey. We wish you all the best as you advance your future!

All the best,

Linda

Introduction

By Ari Ne'eman

College campuses and higher-education settings have a long history as sites of community-building, resistance, and social change. As post-secondary students, you are powerful and empowered self-advocates. You are *not* future-activists, would-be activists, or activists-in-training—you are activists *right now* and valued members of the larger disability advocacy community.

This handbook gives you the tools you need to become a more effective self-advocate, activist, and disability rights advocate. In this handbook, you will find in-depth information on establishing a disability advocacy group at your school, organizing meetings and events, navigating disability and mental health services, and ensuring that disabled students have a voice on campus.

For the past several decades, the disability rights movement has been promoting the social model of disability and advancing the causes of dignity, self-determination, and community integration for all people with all disabilities. As self-advocates, we join our allies across various other communities to advance the rights of all disabled people, and we focus on addressing issues that specifically affect the disability community, such as the lack of community-based supports and services for disabled adults, damaging rhetoric which paints disability as a "disease" and a "burden," and attaining equal access to educational and employment opportunities.

An important part of our work as self-advocates is also the recognition and celebration of disability culture. While attaining the support, accommodations, and respect that we need to thrive within our communities is tremendously important, it is only one aspect of disability activism. As disability activists, we are also members of vibrant communities with our own special customs, vocabulary, and social practices. Disability culture remains dynamic and diverse as more people come together to share and contribute to it. This is an important function of disability-rights groups on college campuses and in other academic environments: bringing individuals together to find their voice, connect with each other, and connect with their larger community.

The lifeblood of national advocacy movements is in the effort and dedication of individual activists working together to reach out to their local communities. Often the process of feeling empowered to talk back to and change one's larger community means carving out safe spaces and firmly requesting accommodation in spaces designed by and for non-disabled people. Safe spaces for the disability community allow disabled people to connect with each other beyond the gaze and interference of non-disabled bystanders. By definition they provide a space in which each individual can feel totally secure and in which everyone can regroup and recharge from inaccessible spaces.

Making spaces not designed with disability in mind fundamentally safe and comfortable for disabled people may require accommodations that may never occur to non-disabled or neurotypical people. Among the wealth of content in this handbook, we have provided information on how to determine the difference between reasonable and unreasonable accommodations and how to request reasonable accommodation in order to make the most of your educational experience and effectively share disability culture and activism on your campus.

The Autistic Self Advocacy Network is honored to join The Daniel Jordan Fiddle Foundation in bringing you this resource and equipping the next generation of leaders in the disability rights movement. This handbook is a clear, detailed guide to help you build a strong community of disability activists at your school, practice effective self-advocacy, and ensure that the legacy of disability advocacy continues long after you have graduated. On behalf of the Autistic Self Advocacy Network and The Daniel Jordan Fiddle Foundation, we wish you the best of luck as you continue to grow as activists and self-advocates.

Organizing

Disability Student Groups and Event Planning
By Allegra Stout

Since I started college, campus disability rights organizing has been one of my most rewarding and enduring activities. As a student with learning disabilities and a history of chronic illness, it has been deeply fulfilling to connect with other disabled students and allies and to work together to create change. In this section, I will share some of the lessons I have learned during three and a half years of founding, building up, leading, and ensuring the sustainability of a disability rights group on a small, private liberal arts campus. (Although my experiences have been in a cross-disability context, most of the lessons I have learned are equally applicable to groups specifically for autistic students or students with another particular disability.)

Starting a group

You may be lucky enough to be at a college that already has a student group focused on disability rights or whatever other area you have in mind. If not, here are some things to consider as you think about starting a group:

Why do you want to have a disability-focused student group? What are your goals, and are certain ones more important or urgent than others? For example, when I was a first-year student, I felt very isolated as a disabled student, because I couldn't find anyone talking about disability, except from the perspectives of volunteer work or, in classes, medical issues. For me, then, developing a sense of disability community was a major goal. Other goals might include increasing understanding of disability issues among students, faculty, and/or staff; improving university policies affecting disabled students; or increasing various types of accessibility around campus. Being clear about your goals will help you communicate with others about the new group.

How can you reach out to potential members? Think creatively about ways to find students who might be interested. You might already have friends or classmates you know to be interested in disability issues. Perhaps your disability services provider would be willing to send an email to students registered with her or his office. You can post fliers around campus and use whatever online tools are available for publicizing student activities. Reaching out to other student groups can also be helpful, both to find new members for your group and to begin developing lasting relationships.

What steps are necessary to officially start a new student group? This varies widely depending on campus policies. At some colleges, new groups need a list of members and a faculty advisor, while at others it's as simple as filling out an online form. Check with your office of student life or student activities, or ask students with more experience to get the details.

Depending on your particular circumstances, including campus policies and whether you are starting out alone or already have a few interested people, you might officially create a group and then start recruitment and meetings, or you might try to get more people involved before formalizing things. Either way, here are some things to think about as your group begins to get off the ground:

Naming your group: The name of your group is important not just because it's often the first thing outsiders encounter, but also because it can convey important information about your values, political beliefs, and goals. For example, my student group is called "Wesleyan Students for Disability Rights." This might seem benign, but it actually has some important implications. First, the group is focused on "Wesleyan Students." We have had several members from the surrounding community who are not Wesleyan students, but we've decided to keep our primary focus within the campus. Second, we are comfortable talking frankly about "Disability." At one point some students within the group suggested that a phrase like "Differently Abled" might be better, but we all discussed it and decided that we want to align ourselves with the broader disability rights movement.

When choosing your name and writing any other materials, another important issue of language is whether to say "students with disabilities" or "disabled students," or to use some combination of the two, or another phrase entirely. (If you are running a disability-specific group, you may still run into similar issues, such as "Autistic students, "autistic students," or "students with autism.") Although the differences between these phrases might seem subtle, they are often extremely important to people.

Before using any of these phrases in an official capacity (such as in the group name), it might be helpful to gather a few interested students to talk about the differences and what you all call yourselves. Try to reach an agreement about what's best for the group (e.g. picking one because most people use it or to make a political point, or alternating back and forth.)

Leadership: "Nothing about us without us" is one of the most famous slogans of the disability rights movement. It means that discussions and work about disability need to be led by disabled people. Non-disabled allies can sometimes play important roles, but disabled people need to set the agenda for matters concerning us. As you start your group and recruit more members, you and the other people involved will need to consider how and to what extent your group will uphold this principle.

One factor to consider is that your college may have policies requiring that student groups, or even leadership roles, be open to all students. This could mean that restricting leadership to disabled students might be considered reverse discrimination. If you are concerned about this, check with your office of student life or student activities.

Also, especially when groups have very few people, you may decide that it doesn't make sense to exclude someone from a leadership role because of disability status. Alternatively, you and your other group members may feel that it's extremely important disabled students lead the group.

As with choosing your name and other language use, this is a good opportunity for a group discussion about your values, political beliefs, and goals, in order to determine what is best for the group. I would caution, however, that if non-disabled students are given leadership roles within the group, it is very important that they be aware of their roles as allies and that they have a good understanding of their non-disabled privilege.

Group structure: As your group gets off the ground, you and the other people involved will need to make decisions about how you will operate and get things done. A lot of this depends on circumstances on your particular campus, such as whether it's residential or commuter, small or large, and overly bureaucratic or more supportive of free-form student organizing. It can be helpful to join other, more established groups on campus in order to see what works and doesn't and how student groups generally operate at your school.

Things to consider include:

- Meetings: Many student groups find that one meeting at the same time every week works well, but figure out what's best for you. You might consider combinations of online or in-person meetings, or having some meetings for planning systems change campaigns and others for getting to know each and talking about your lives.
- Leadership structure: Some student groups have a formal structure, with officers like the president, vice-president, treasurer, and so on. Others share leadership, with roles assigned informally or on a rotating basis. This partly depends on the size of your group, as it may be easier to maintain informal, non-hierarchical structures with small groups.
- Making decisions: It helps to have a sense of how your group will proceed when it's time to decide on priorities, next steps, or responding to incidents on campus. You might discuss issues and then have a majority-rules vote. In my experience, consensus-based decision-making, in which members consider everyone's opinion and try to come to an agreement that works for everyone, has been an effective way of making sure that everyone feels represented and valued.

Setting an Agenda

By Elizabeth Boresow

It is a good idea to have an agenda prepared before you go into each meeting. You may need a specific agenda that addresses a lot of points or you may just need a general agenda. You must consider what your members want in a group if you are going to keep those members!

In order to keep the group enjoyable and productive, it may be nice to have a two-fold purpose in the group. My organization has two types of meetings: advocacy meetings and social meetings. Social meetings require less of an agenda. A social agenda might include introductions, an activity, and then announcements about upcoming activities or the next meeting. The focus is on interactions and having fun! Advocacy meetings are the type of meetings that require a more formal agenda. There should still be introductions at the start and announcements about upcoming activities and meetings at the end, but what happens in between them is more structured.

You should consider the "make-up" of your organization when you set an agenda. Do you have all freshmen or all graduate students or something in between? Will you have others in attendance, such as administration, faculty or staff members, guest speakers, or reporters present?

Your freshmen may want help with the transition to college. This could include leading discussions or role-playing sessions on talking to professors, working with the Disability Resources office, navigating the University web site, or figuring out the wheelchair-accessible routes on campus. You could put a time in the meeting for younger members (or older students with recently acquired disabilities) to ask questions of your more experienced members.

Depending on your University, the group may want to make improving campus accessibility a priority (this could be either physical accessibility or policy accessibility or both). See chapter three for more information on how to make this happen. In a meeting, you could put in an item (topic for discussion) on the barriers your members are experiencing and if you would like to do something to improve the system.

Another area for discussion in a meeting, if you so choose, is collaborative planning. There may be other student groups you could team up with to host events. You may want to host events on your own. Have a discussion about the kind of events you would like to host and who you might want to host them with. For example, you could host a self-defense class with an instructor who is willing to work with people of all abilities. Another sort of collaboration is for similar goals. Our organization has teamed up with Queers and Allies and the Women's Resource Center on a task force to improve the restroom facilities at our University.

Consider this description of a social meeting that took place in our group last semester. Group members helped arrange carpools for those coming from student housing dormitories and apartments. Everybody met at a restaurant off-campus and arranged tables outside for the meeting. The outdoor location helped the sound from the conversations spread out more, which was important for some members. People were free to order and eat or to just sit with the group. After those who got food had brought it outside, everybody took a minute to introduce themselves by stating their name, year, major, and role in the group or disability community. Our student group was visited at this meeting by our University's new ADA Coordinator. She had the opportunity to ask us questions about our group and we had the opportunity to ask her about her transition into a new position. From there, we all simply enjoyed eating together and talking about how our semesters were going. After some social chatting, we talked about group events: we made sure we had successfully completed thank-you notes to visitors we had brought to teach an inclusive self-defense class and we talked about upcoming speaking engagements and assigned certain members to different classes. After this, we left tips for our waitress and made sure everybody had a ride back to where they needed to go.

Consider this description of a typical advocacy meeting from our student group. Members who are in charge of various projects will come with updates about the status of the project. These meetings tend to take place in a campus building around a table. Sometimes, we will have University administration join us for the second half of a meeting if we need to discuss something with them. First, the group will go in a circle and everybody will introduce themselves with their name, year, major, and role in the organization or disability community. Then the president or vice-president will lead the group in updates about various projects (which could include bringing in guest speakers, sending out speakers, group campfires or game nights), notification of other related University information (such as the Student Union Activities group bringing in a comedian with a disability), member successes, concerns with campus accessibility (such as a door opener at the health center being broken or a teacher making inappropriate comments), and brainstorming to hear what members are interested in doing as a group. If the group is meeting with University administration, the beginning of the meeting (before the administrator arrives) may be used also to review the main points we want to communicate with the administrator. In that case, the last half of a meeting may involve administrators and provide a chance to the group members who want to stay to practice advocacy skills and relay both gratitude and concerns to the University as well as receive updates on what their side is doing. At the conclusion of these meetings, a leader will reiterate the next few items on the group calendar and make sure everybody has a ride back to where they need to be. These meetings often end with members deciding to go out to dinner together or have dinner in the dormitory cafeteria together.

When setting a meeting agenda, consider the needs of possible attendees in order to make the meeting as accessible as possible. When our organization sends out emails about upcoming meetings, we include a statement that asks those with accommodations needs to email us so we can prepare materials. In this way, we will be able to secure an interpreter, large-print materials, or whatever other needs somebody may have. In addition to those needs that require preparation before the meeting, consider the needs of people during the meeting. Our meetings take place in a variety of locations, but members know they are free to get up and take a break if they need. People are welcome to bring computers, paper and pen, earplugs, service animals, food or whatever supplies will assist them in participating successfully in a meeting. Copies of the meeting agenda can be emailed to those using screen readers and print copies can be distributed at a meeting to help attendees understand the schedule for the meeting. Finally, consider giving every person the opportunity to speak, as some may struggle with when it is appropriate for them to participate. During this time, it should be expressed that people are free to "pass" and just listen.

Use these examples as a guide. They are not the only possibilities for how group meetings an be shaped, but they may offer you some general suggestions while you prepare a meeting agenda.

Whether the goal of your meeting is primarily social or advocacy-related, knowing your goals will help you set an agenda that addresses the needs of your members.

EXAMPLE PAPER AGENDA:

disAbility Student Group
Anonymous University
Tuesday, July 3, 2012
Building XYZ

- Group Introductions (Name, Year, Major, Position in Group/Disability Community)
- Publicity Update
  - Vote on t-shirt design (Lisa)
  - health center needs more brochures for our group (Greg)
  - How to recruit freshmen (brainstorm)
- Advocacy Update
  - Article in newspaper (who can meet with reporter next week?)
  - Summary of last meeting with University administrators (Emily)
  - Teaching class needs 2-4 speakers for a panel (Tuesday night in April)
- Programming/Service Update
  - Plans & logistics for bringing in self-defense instructor (Parker)
  - Audio Reader needs volunteers
  - Group volunteering at homeless shelter (sign up now)
- Elections for group next year (Casey)
- Wrap Up
  - Any accessibility concerns? (broken elevators, damaged sidewalks, websites not working with JAWS, trouble with teachers/staff)
  - Improvements to acknowledge? (fixed desk heights, installed flashing doorbell...)
  - Next social event: Bowling (date/time/arrange rides)
  - Next advocacy meeting (date/time/arrange rides)
  - Web site will have dates, times & locations of future group activities

Thanks for coming!

Planning Successful Events
By Allegra Stout

Once you get a few folks together, you will probably want to start planning events to share your interests with other students and community members. Film screenings, guest speakers, workshops, protests, teach-ins, parties, and discussion groups are just a few of the types of events you can use to increase understanding of disability and social justice on campus and to create change in specific areas.

When planning events, it's important to think carefully about:

- What exactly will happen
- Time and date
- Location
- Advertising
- Food
- Money
- Accessibility

In my experience it has usually helped to designate one or two people to "bottom-line" the event. This means that, although many people may be handling various aspects of the vent planning, those one or two people will oversee everything, check in with people to make sure things are getting done, take care of any loose ends, and ensure the overall smoothness of the event.

At every stage of the event-planning process, the levels of bureaucracy and paperwork (or online forms) depend on the way things work at your particular school. I will try to give general guidelines below, but be prepared to modify them to suit the processes that make sense for you. For advice and procedures, check with your student government, student activities office, and/or more experienced student organizers.

Collaborations
The first step in event planning is usually to decide what will happen, and when. Depending on the type of event, this could including contacting an outside speaker, discussing within the group what days are best for a discussion, choosing student presenters for a workshop, and/or making sure that you will be able to get the screening rights for a film. When choosing a date, try to avoid conflicting with other events if possible.

When choosing a location, you will need to estimate how many people you think will attend. This can be hard to judge, but make your best guess based on similar past events organized by your group or other groups, the type of event (e.g., a workshop will probably draw fewer people than a movie screening), and the intensity with which you will be advertising. In some cases, you may decide to limit attendance, such as if you require pre-registration for a training or only invite certain student groups. Make sure that your location is as accessible as possible. If some buildings on your campus are not ADA-accessible, it is probably best to avoid them entirely, especially for events open to the public. Also keep in mind factors like ambient noise, scents, and transportation complications.

After you plan the type of event, the time, and the location, you will need to advertise! How far in advance you should advertise your event depends on how things are usually done at your school. On my campus, student events are rarely advertised more than a week or two in advance. By the time information needs to start going out, though, you should already have a plan for exactly how (what media and when) you will advertise and who will be responsible for each task. Common types of advertising include blogs, official university calendars, listservs for student groups, fliers around campus, ads in student newspapers, Facebook events, mailings, personal emails, emails to academic departments, announcements in classes and at other events, and word of mouth.

The intensity of your advertising campaign will depend on the type of event. For a major public speaker or performer, you may want to attract as large an audience as possible and thus should use all available means of advertising, early and often. But for social justice workshop designed for people who are already involved in campus activism, you may want to focus your advertising more on student group listservs and personal invitations.

Many types of advertising work best when they have a personal touch, because people will be more interested if they feel connected to the source. For example, you can email administrative assistants of random academic departments to ask them to send out emails, but it will be even better if members of your group majoring in those departments contact them. Likewise, emails to student listservs will likely be more effective if they come from someone who has been actively involved in that student community. (This is one area where your relationships with other student groups can come in handy!) Accordingly, word of mouth is one of the most effective advertising techniques. If everyone in your group has conversations with their friends explaining just how awesome the upcoming event will be and why this particular friend should care about it, you will probably get a much higher turnout. My favorite technique, in fact, is first to saturate the campus with ads of various kinds, and then to follow-up with personal conversations along the lines of, "Hey, did you see the flyers for that disabled woman of color spoken word artist's performance next Saturday at 8? I've been working on bringing her to campus, and it would mean a lot to me if you could come. Plus, I've seen some of her videos on YouTube and I think you'll really like her, especially since you've been working on those poems about Puerto Rican identity for your English class."

Food is often a strong motivator for attending events, especially for people who are mildly interested but don't yet have a strong investment in the topic. Providing food could mean anything from ordering dinner from a local restaurant to requesting catering from the campus food supplier to baking some brownies. Whatever you decided (and get funding for!), be sure to advertise it. Also be careful to build in time for people to fill their plates and eat, if it's more than just snacks.

Money
Events vary widely in how much they cost. If it's just you and other members of your group leading a workshop in a room in the campus center, you may not need any funding at all, or perhaps just a few dollars to buy snacks. At the other extreme, if you're flying in several performers from across the country, you may need thousands of dollars for their airfare, taxis, hotels, and honoraria

(payments). When you do determine that you need funding for an event or other project, start by making a list of exactly what you will need it for and how much everything costs. It may be impossible to do this fully, as sometimes you will need to request funding before you've finished negotiating honoraria or determined exact catering prices, but use your best estimates.

Next, find out about funding sources on your campus, and then request what you need. As with everything else, you can seek advice from your student government, student activities office, and/or more experienced student organizers. Some common sources of funding include student governments, certain fraternities, student activities offices, academic departments, and perhaps even the disability services office. Each funding source may have different restrictions. For example, on my campus the student government is a great source of large amounts of money for events, but never funds food. The student activities office, on the other hand, is happy to give money for food, but usually limits it to $200. It may help to keep a list of funding sources, their requirements, and the procedures and deadlines for requesting money. (This will also help with group sustainability, as the knowledge won't just disappear when you or other leaders graduate!)

Try to think creatively about funding, and find ways to make your event seem appealing and relevant to funding sources that might not seem obvious. For example, my group has hosted guest lectures about the neurodiversity movement. Our campus health center has a fund for student events that are related to health and well-being, so I successfully made the case that educating the campus about neurodiversity would create a more inclusive and affirming environment for Autistic students and others with non-normative neurologies. Finding the health center's fund in the first place, though, took a lot of asking staff and more experienced students, and poking around on university web pages.

Collaborations can be vital for securing enough funding for major events. Funding sources may be more willing to help you when they see that there are several groups working to make an event happen and that it will be of interest to a wide audience. You may need to pull together money from a variety of sources and groups' budgets to reach your goals.

I've found working with Residential Life staff to be extraordinarily helpful in event planning. At my school, and perhaps at yours too, all Resident Advisors are required to hold several events each semester, and they have small budgets for doing so. In order for events to count, several of their residents must attend. When I am planning major events, I have an RA friend email their listserv asking for volunteers, and sometimes get as many as 10 responses. If each of these RAs contributes a few dollars and brings a few residents, the event is much better funded and reaches a much wider audience than it would otherwise. Plus, while it may be best for your group members to keep control of delicate tasks like communicating with guest speakers, RAs are great for things like advertising, arranging food, and requesting funding. Keep in mind, though, that collaborations of all kinds may actually increase your workload or that of other event organizers, despite bringing in more people to help out. Someone will need to delegate tasks, check in with everyone to make sure everything is getting done, put people in touch with one another, organize planning meetings, and (as I said earlier) generally bottom-line the event. (I've found shared online spreadsheets, like GoogleDocs, very helpful for coordinating tasks and tracking progress.) Still, working with people outside your group can have wonderful short-term and long-term benefits and is usually worth the extra effort.

Accessibility: Last but not least, accessibility should be a major part of every event planning process. You should consider accessibility in every aspect and at every stage of your planning. Accessibility isn't just important for the room where you hold the actual event, but is also vital for the rooms where you hold planning meetings, the hotel where you host guest lecturers or performers, any transportation involved, your advertising, food, and much more. Also, accessibility goes beyond making sure that people with varying abilities can participate. Depending on the context, you may also need to consider financial accessibility, accessibility for people with children, accessibility for people with various dietary restrictions, and other ways of including everyone.

I won't try to provide an exhaustive list of ways in which things should be accessible. For that, talk to people with various disabilities on your campus and beyond, consult with your disability services provider, and research what other groups are doing for accessibility. Instead, I'll point out a few things that are particularly important when planning events.

It's important to include accessibility information in your advertising. This will help take the burden off of individuals to find out for themselves if they'll be able to participate and will show that you're considering everyone's needs. On your fliers and Facebook events, state whether the building is physically accessible, what kinds of food will be provided, the cost of the event (or if it's free), whether there will be childcare, and so on. If you can't provide certain types of accessibility (such as if you really tried to find a room without fluorescent lights but just weren't able to manage it this time), it's better to say so upfront, so that people can make informed decisions about their participation. You can also include a statement asking people not to wear scented products, so that people with multiple chemical sensitivities can attend.

It also helps to designate an access "point person." Advertise this person's contact information, so that potential attendees have someone to contact if they have questions or requests regarding accessibility. (Keep privacy concerns in mind: your point person may want to use a group email address, rather than a personal one, and an office phone number, if you have one, rather than a personal cell number.) The point person can also be responsible for making sure access needs are met on the day of the event.

Many types of accessibility take some advance preparation, such as hiring a sign language interpreter or creating large-print versions of documents. It can help to include a sentence along the lines of "Please let us know of any access needs at least 48 hours in advance" with the point person's contact information, so that potential attendees know that you want to work with them to ensure access and so that you have time to do so.

As I mentioned, access goes beyond disability-specific needs. Making your event free or cheap will enable more people to attend. Depending on your campus community and whether the event is open to the public, childcare may also be important. (Childcare doesn't need to be expensive; see if you can organize a few volunteers. But also be sure to check with your school for any rules regarding liability.) You can also help increase safety for transgender and gender-nonconforming people by holding your event in a building with gender-neutral or single-use bathrooms or pointing out where the nearest ones are.

When planning for accessibility, especially for a public event, thinking expansively is a form of activism and creating change. Don't limit yourself to the types of access needs that you know people on your campus or in your group definitely have or to the level of accessibility required by the Americans with Disabilities Act or other laws. Increasing accessibility can expand attendees' awareness and understanding of diverse needs and spark them to make their own projects more accessible. It also demonstrates your commitment to inclusion and creates a more welcoming environment.

To give one example, my group recently hosted a performer who asked that we try to make her event accessible for people with multiple chemical sensitivities (MCS). We had never discussed MCS, and to the best of our knowledge no events at our school had ever tried achieve scent-free spaces. But, realizing the importance of taking a stand for access, we did our best. We placed scent-free soap in the restrooms, marked off a scent-free seating area and worked with the ushers to help audience members understand its purpose, and, at the recommendation of the performer, included this statement in our advertising:

> **Access Info:** We will have scent-free seating and maintain clear laneways for those who use wheelchairs & other access devices. Please do not take flash photography, and please do not wear perfumes, colognes or essential oils. We will have scent-free soaps in the washrooms (but we cannot guarantee a scent-free space). Please email [my email address] with any access concerns/questions/needs.

At the actual event, many audience members probably were not scent-free, and only one person sat in the scent-free area. Even if no one had sat there, though, I would consider this a meaningful advance toward an accessible campus. We exposed many people to the concept of scent-free spaces and got them started thinking about that type of access. If we do this enough, other campus groups may start to make similar efforts, and we will create a safer environment for community members, current or future, with MCS.

Conclusion

I hope that the lessons I have learned will help you or at least give you food for thought in your campus organizing. If my advice doesn't work for you, though, don't despair. Every campus and every group is different, and part of the excitement of organizing is thinking outside the box to do whatever works for your community, where you are, with what you have. There are many resources available to help, including this guide, your classmates, and your campus administrators, but ultimately, through trial and error and persistence, you will forge your own path for change.

Conference Planning

By Alex Umstead

Symposiums are an excellent venue for students to gather to present their innovative ideas and to have meaningful discussions about their topics of interest. There are many ways to conduct and organize a symposium. The following is an example of how one might go about planning and setting up a symposium in a university setting:

In August 2011, Syracuse University hosted a symposium on neurodiversity and autistic self-advocacy. As the symposium coordinator and a first-time conference planner, I was asked to write a short paper on conference planning. In this paper, I outline a number of issues—both positive and negative—that I encountered while working on the symposium and provide suggestions to assist other individuals organizing such events for the first time in planning their events efficiently.

At the time the neurodiversity symposium occurred in 2011, various members of the planning committee and I had been working on the event since October 2009. We had originally planned on having the symposium one to two months later than we did, but changed the date to Friday, August 5th, in order to make it coincide with a larger conference that was set to occur that same weekend so that travel would be easier for individuals who were going to be present at both conferences. Don't worry if your ideas or focus change during the time you're planning the conference; as long as you have enough time to organize what you need to in order to make your ideas work, changing things up can sometimes be a good thing. The idea I had during my senior year of college that evolved into the neurodiversity symposium was radically different from what the event became in its final incarnation. While the final symposium was a 7-hour event that consisted of a keynote by Ari Ne'eman (president of the Autistic Self-Advocacy Network) and four presentations, I had originally envisioned nothing more than having someone from Syracuse University do a short lunchtime seminar on neurodiversity for students and staff at SUNY ESF, the institution I received my bachelor's from (SUNY ESF is an environmental science-focused state school located next to the Syracuse University campus). This idea did not change until after I had emailed out a request for assistance with planning it to the listserv for a disability advocacy group at SU. After meeting with an individual who responded to my email, we decided to bring Ari in and have the event at Syracuse University itself, as the SU School of Education has a long history of promoting social justice for individuals with disabilities. (We ended up tabling the idea for presenting at ESF indefinitely due to a lack of ability on my part to commit the time necessary for doing so.) We were continuing to switch up which panels we wanted to happen at the symposium just weeks before it happened—although I would not recommend doing this, as it forced us to cut down the number of panels we were originally going to have.

Another suggestion I would make with regard to this same topic would be to create a draft agenda as soon as you are sure (or relatively sure) of who will be presenting at what points during your event and what topics they will be presenting on. We did not have a finalized agenda until less than two weeks before the event, unfortunately, so panelists had to prepare their presentations relatively quickly. Make sure to get input from all individuals working on your conference—especially speakers—in order to ensure that both the timing of events at the conference and the date of the conference itself do not conflict with anyone's schedule. Before moving the neurodiversity symposium to August 5th, we had already moved the date around multiple times because of scheduling conflicts different speakers had.

As a first-time conference planner, make sure you don't have to do everything yourself. Don't be afraid to ask for help! While the neurodiversity symposium had a wonderful planning committee, it was difficult to find meeting times that all of our members were able to attend. If you become distracted easily or have difficulty organizing people or ideas, having other people around who are able to refocus the conversation, when necessary, can be a real plus. Make sure to communicate with other members of your planning group—and do so clearly—so that everybody is kept up to date on the progress of your event. Have clear goals for what you want your event to address. If you have co-planners who are more knowledgeable about the subject of your conference (or aspects of it) than you are, listen to the suggestions they make. This does not mean that you must implement every one of these suggestions—but it does give you an advantage in figuring out what might work best for achieving the goals you desire from your event.

Make sure to know your costs and contributors! Have people on your board who know how to figure out a budget and can help determine which ways would be best to raise sufficient funds for supporting your conference. Find out what your speakers charge for presenting at events and how they charge (per hour, per event, etc.) Depending on how you are running your conference and how large it is, you may only have to pay honoraria to some speakers and not others. In some cases, speakers will waive honoraria. Make sure that you obtain cost estimates for other things such as conference space, catering, travel expenses for speakers, printing materials, and ordering items (such as t-shirts) to sell at the event. It is also important to ensure that you know where your funding will be coming from and how much you will be getting from each source. Make a bank account specifically for your event. This may be relatively easy to do in a university setting. However, we did run into one difficulty: while we had secured money from various departments at SU for the symposium, some of the departments that had agreed to fund us could not transfer money to our account without obtaining a list of items that their funding would go toward. This was compounded by the fact that we did not know all of our costs until right before or after the symposium.

Make sure you advertise!!! We set up a blog for the symposium (http://neurodiversitysymposium.wordpress.com), hung up posters, sent out notices to email lists, and sold tshirts online. If you have a specific website or blog page for your event (which would be a good idea), try and make sure that your page is accessible to individuals who use software that translates on-screen text to audio (such as JAWS or Window-Eyes). While there are sites online that allow you to check accessibility features of websites, it is always best to have someone knowledgeable in screen-reading programs—preferably an individual who ordinarily relies on them for accessing their computer's interface—to verify that your page is accessible.

In addition, it is important to ensure that you get your facts correct when creating anything meant for public consumption, since if the event you are planning deals with any issue that is potentially controversial, some individuals may take issue with the definitions used in your event or criticize the event itself. While most of the publicity we received online was positive, there were a few individuals opposed to neurodiversity who posted links to the event and wrote disparagingly about what we were going to do there. One individual in particular, someone known for making virulent attacks online against neurodiversity and Ari in particular, had registered for the symposium and advertised his intention to attend the event and cause a disruption during Ari's keynote presentation. If you are planning an event for the first time, dealing with a situation like this could be very anxiety-provoking.

In most cases, there is no reason to respond to individuals who act in this way; if you must respond, never do so in a confrontational way. Remember that every blogger with a vendetta against your cause could repost what you say online and twist it to reflect negatively on you. If you are unsure about what to do, look for advice from people higher up than you, who may have dealt with situations like this before (I contacted faculty in my department), in order to get advice on the situation. If you are worried about the safety of anyone at your event, contact the security staff at your sponsoring institution beforehand to inform them of the situation. Your ability to prevent disruptions at your event may vary depending on what kind of venue you are planning an event for. As SU is a private institution, and their campus private property, the university would have been able to simply kick this individual off of campus for being disruptive; however, all universities may not have the ability to do this.

Lastly, it is important to make sure that your conference itself is as universally accessible as possible. At a bare minimum, ask anyone registering if they have any required accommodations or dietary needs , and ensure that the location of your event is in compliance with the Americans with Disabilities Act. However, in the spirit of universal accessibility, it is also important to look at additional needs that people may have, such as being in a room without fluorescent lighting or being able to leave the room for periods of time without feeling like they are interrupting a lecture or activity.

Despite the challenges the other planners and I faced when planning the 2011 Neurodiversity Symposium, the event went well and was very enjoyable and informative. We are currently looking to make the Symposium an ongoing event at Syracuse University occurring once every year or two. I hope that any of you who are also stressing (but hopefully excited!) about planning a conference for the first time will see similar success!

Sustaining Your Group: How to Make Sure Things Keep Going Once You've Left College

By Melanie Yergeau

Forming a student group requires dedication, time, and patience. From locating members and seeking out faculty advisors to planning events and educating your fellow students, maintaining a student group involves a good deal of personal investment. This issue of time commitment is one that I offer from personal experience. When I was a student at Ohio State, I formed a student chapter of the Autistic Self Advocacy Network (ASAN). Deciding what our group would look like and planning our first meeting, for example, took several months of work.

And yet, despite the energy required, running a disability advocacy group is a highly fulfilling venture — a rewarding experience to which other authors here, including Allegra and Elizabeth, have attested. For my own part, I directed ASAN-Ohio State for nearly two years. I wouldn't trade that experience for the world. Our student group has made a tangible, real difference in the lives of many people (including my own). Because of my leadership experiences, I've become a stronger self-advocate, a member of a powerful community, and a person who's more confident and comfortable as an Autistic activist. What's more, our group has combatted a lot of ignorance regarding disability. We've held protests, disability pride events, and talks with undergraduate classes and faculty across the university. If it weren't for our group, our campus community probably wouldn't know that Autistic culture even *exists*.

I offer the above narrative because it highlights an important, pressing issue: the need to keep our disability groups going once we're gone. The further I delved into my studies, the more I realized that, one day, I wouldn't be at Ohio State any more… and who was going to take over the chapter that I'd spent so many hours co-building? What would happen to student disability advocacy once I graduated?

It's a scary thought, in a lot of ways, to realize that disability groups might fizzle out once their leaders are gone. And, unfortunately, this sort of turnover is common across student organizations of all kinds — it's not just limited to disability groups. I think what makes our situation unique, though, is that our groups are often the *only* disability advocacy groups that exist at a given college or university. At large universities, for example, there might be several groups dedicated to chess, or world hunger, or politics, or dance parties. But it's unlikely for there to be multiple advocacy groups led by disabled students. Often, the disability groups that *do* exist are charity-driven, run by well-meaning but woefully ill-informed and non-disabled students. While I was at Ohio State, for instance, there was only one other group run by disabled students: a cross-disability group that stopped holding meetings because they couldn't find replacements for their student leaders.

As you can imagine, advocacy groups led by disabled students are sorely needed. They help us find and build community. They enable us to fight oppression and discrimination. They allow us to make systems change. They encourage us to take pride in who we are as disabled people. So, the question is: What can we do? How can we ensure that our groups outlive us?

I don't pretend to have all the answers here. Sustaining a chapter is tricky business, and a lot depends on context—the type of university you attend (a small liberal arts college? a community college? a large, state-run university?), the resources available to you (willing students? faculty? money? time?), and the community outside your university walls (are you in an urban area? rural? a place with accessible transportation?). What I can offer are some suggestions, things I'd advise you to think about early in your organization's development. The longevity of your group depends on your revisiting these issues regularly and *throughout* its lifespan.

1. Recruit new members—continually

One of the first things discussed in this handbook was the importance of finding members. In order to have a group, you need to have, well, a group! However, many student groups make a large mistake—once they locate an initial membership, they stop looking for new people. As a result, by the time late spring rolls around, their membership has dried up. Some people graduate or move on, and the remaining group members may disband because the group has grown too small for comfort. This sort of thing happens more often than people realize. Members migrate and then don't return, and the group ceases to exist.

Once you've built a solid membership base, don't stop. Keep looking for new and eager people. You might, for example, appoint someone as the Recruiting Coordinator for your group. That person could take responsibility for hosting a table at student involvement fairs or university events; they might even send emails, post flyers on bulletin boards, or set up on the campus lawn and hand out brochures.

2. Delegate tasks

This might sound corny or silly, but the moment you start a group, you should begin grooming your potential successors. When we build advocacy groups from the ground up, we often get very attached to them—and sometimes have a tendency to do *way* too much of the work needed to keep the group going. We forget that ours is a collective, group effort rather than a one-person show. I'm the first to admit my guilt here—I have difficulty knowing when I should ask other people to assist me. Plus, I can't help feeling a little bit parental about the things I create. What helped me, though, was thinking about our student group this way: If I kept doing everything, then nobody else would know what to do once I left. And then the group would fizzle out and die.

Once you start holding meetings, identify people who are willing to contribute. In addition to locating officers (e.g., a treasurer, secretary, etc.), you might also form committees for various tasks or events. Figure out where people's interests and strengths lie, and then capitalize on those for the betterment of your group. Additionally, make sure that there are *at least* one or two people who know how to do the things you do—whether that's running a meeting, sending out emails, balancing the budget, or planning an event. It's important that others know how to sustain the group so that, once your time comes to an end, you don't hurriedly have to find and train replacements.

3. Develop co-mentoring relationships

Even though student groups usually operate under a hierarchical structure (president, vice president, treasurer, etc.), it's important *not* to limit your group to this hierarchy. That is, your group should not be a one-person, two-person, or three-person show—its direction and scope shouldn't be directed solely by a handful of officers.

Here I want to suggest two things: mentor others in your group, and ask others to mentor you. I think it's here important to understand co-mentoring not as an expert/novice relationship, but rather as a relationship that involves give and take from both parties. In a student disability organization, co-mentoring might take many shapes. It might involve the delegation issues that I suggested above in section #2. You might, for example, form committees and charge each member with taking responsibility for a certain topic, area, or task; and those committees could then interface or collaborate with other committees, sharing their ideas, knowledge, and work with one another.

But co-mentoring might also involve befriending new group members, meeting one another for coffee and talking about non-group related things, or sending emails to one another about issues that are important to you. The key is developing relationships with each other beyond a framework of teacher/student or helper/helpee. Recognizing every member, regardless of age or experience, as an asset with something important to share is essential to maintaining a cohesive, long-running group in which everyone feels welcome and valued.

4. Develop relationships with other campus groups or centers

Upon forming ASAN-Ohio State, we quickly realized the importance of collaborating with other entities on campus. In part, collaboration was necessary for the success of the events we hosted— seeking funding from Student Life, asking the Disability Studies program to help us advertise, reserving room space from the English Department, receiving administrative help from the university's developmental disability center, and so forth. Without support from other campus units, our group wouldn't have accomplished much, nor would it have lasted very long.

However, campus relationships involve more than simply asking others for their support— relationships also involve lending your own support. In short, be good stewards to your campus community. For our student group, this came in a number of forms. For instance, many of us volunteered to visit social work and disability studies classes, where we talked with students about self-advocacy and disability rights. Each fall, we'd also send representatives to beginning-of-the-year events hosted by the Office of Disability Services and programs through the Nisonger Center, and we'd lend our support as mentors to new students and community members.

5. Find sponsorship outside the university

This, I think, is a good thought to end on regarding sustainability. Colleges can be insular places. When I was an undergrad, students often referred to our campus as The Giant Bubble. When your university is in a small town or rural area—and especially when you don't have access to transportation—cultivating relationships *beyond* campus walls can be quite the challenge.

Our student group encountered many difficulties when we began developing community relationships. The vast majority of our group consisted of non-drivers, and, on top of that, none of us relished the thought of socializing with strangers. We did, however, have certain resources available to us. Some group members were originally from Columbus and had personal connections with other disability groups. And other members had friends, professors, or family members with connections. Our first group meetings, then, involved a lot of list-making—determining who knew who and how we might begin to network and capitalize on those relationships. We made our initial contacts through email, and, so far, our student group has collaborated or been in contact with a number of local disability groups and agencies.

In addition to cultivating community relationships, you might also begin to think about your student group and its place within a *national* (or even *international*) disability community. A group's longevity depends on stability, and a national disability group might lend some of that stability. So, you might consider the following: Would it make sense to affiliate your student group with a larger disability organization? In our group's case, we became a chapter of ASAN—a move that has proven invaluable. Affiliating with another disability group doesn't guarantee sustainability, but doing so might provide your group with professional mentoring, a known reputation, nonprofit work experience, and/or external funding.

Service Provision and Accommodation

<u>What are Schools Required to do Under the Law?</u>
By Melanie Yergeau

If you have a disability, it's very likely that you've encountered the phrase reasonable accommodation at some point in your school or work life. Under the Americans with Disabilities Act (ADA), students have a legal right to said accommodations in classroom contexts. These accommodations can take myriad forms, ranging from extended test time to real-time captioning to the use of a computer for test-taking. Perhaps the most important word in this paragraph, however, is the word reasonable. Accommodations must be reasonable; they must not alter the essential nature of a class or cause undue hardship on the part of an employer or university.

For many students with disabilities, reasonableness represents a vast gray area. Our own perceptions of what is reasonable may (and often do) starkly differ from that of our universities. Disability services offices may insist upon standard, formulaic accommodations, accommodations that they provide only for certain disabilities. A student with dyslexia, for example, might receive access to screen reading technology and extended test time, but might be denied accommodation requests that involve alternate forms of class participation. Similarly, an autistic student might receive accommodations that allow for test-taking in a quiet room, but might be denied accommodation requests that involve real-time captioning. This isn't to say, however, that alternative accommodation requests aren't possible - they certainly are. But, generally speaking, a process of negotiation ensues, one that requires you to dialogue with disability services and sometimes professors or other college offices as well.

As an example of this negotiation process - as well as the problemed nature of reasonableness as a concept - I'd like to offer a personal narrative. I'm autistic, and I have documentation attesting my disability and some of the challenges I encounter in school and workplace environments. These documents also provide suggestions for reasonable accommodations. When I was a graduate student, my disability services counselor heavily emphasized the word reasonable. As the ADA notes, if an accommodation is perceived to alter the nature or rigor of an assignment or course, that accommodation can be denied.

Perhaps because of this daunting emphasis on "reasonableness," I didn't seek out accommodations until I was a PhD student - nearly seven years into my college experience. The reasons are manifold, but the primary reason had to do with shame: I was trained to be shameful of my need for "special" requests, trained to be shameful for the ways in which I communicate, process, and create meaning. In short, I was trained to believe that what I needed in order to learn was not reasonable.

Once I did begin to request accommodations, I encountered further difficulties with the notion of what was "reasonable" in the classroom. Because of my difficulties with nonverbals and auditory processing, one of my accommodation requests was a more orderly face-to-face system for class discussions, one in which I might raise my hand or type something on my laptop and show it to another person, who would then read my writing aloud for me. But this particular request was not always well received. For example, in one class I took, a professor refused to call on raised hands because he felt it interrupted the "natural flow of conversation." Two weeks before the term ended, the disability services office managed to convince this professor that my request didn't lessen the rigor of the class. While it's laudable that I received this accommodation in the end, it came too late - materializing only as the class was ending.

I relate this anecdote in order to make a point: I am no longer a student. In fact, I've just completed my first year as a college professor. And in my time as both a student and teacher, I've come to experience the following: accommodation requests are activist work. Universities and employers often have differences in opinion about what the "essential functions" of a job or class mean - in large part because institutions lend their focus to material and economic concerns, often at the expense of inclusion and wide-scale change. When we request accommodations ("reasonable" or not), we disturb (pun intended) the order of the university. And, as such, it's important that we perceive our accommodation requests as more than a singular act. For instance, even though my request for extended time on my PhD candidacy exams enabled me to complete the exam in an equitable manner, my request also paved the way for other students to make similar accommodations. Every request has a ripple effect; it doesn't concern just one student, but rather has the potential to affect many students. And, beyond this, our requests have the potential to instigate wider curricular and institutional change. The more we disclose, request accommodations, and demand such change, the more equal access will become a lived reality.

What are Schools Required to do Under the Law?

By Elizabeth Boresow

Many people who receive "help" growing up in the school system benefit from services mandated by the Individuals with Disabilities Education Act (IDEA). Others are simply helped along by teachers who, realizing some students need an extra hand or a slightly altered approach, make a difference. No matter what one experiences in school growing up, postsecondary institutions promise to be a different experience.

Any sort of postsecondary educational institution (whether it be a college, University, or technical school) is required to follow a different set of standards. The Rehabilitation Act of 1973 and the Americans with Disabilities Act of 1990 (ADA) are federal laws that protect the idea of equal access for people with disabilities. The ADA has several sections.

Title I prohibits discrimination against people with disabilities in all aspects of employment. This means one cannot refuse to hire someone just because the person has a disability, fire somebody solely because that person has a disability, or refuse to train somebody or give that person pay raises simply because of a disability. This means applicants with disabilities must be considered and treated like all other applicants: based on their ability to do the job. One cannot inquire about a disability unless it interferes with the applicant's ability to do the job.

Title II says that local and state facilities must follow regulations set in place by the Department of Justice to ensure accessibility of physical facilities and the services they provide. If a school receives any federal funding, it falls into this category. Some examples of qualifying schools are state schools and community colleges.

Title III says that people with disabilities cannot be discriminated against by a place of public accommodation. This means they must have reasonable access to the goods, services, and facilities of such places. These places include hotels, stores, daycare centers, and gyms. Educational facilities that fall under this title include private schools that do not receive federal funding.

Title IV involves equal access to telecommunication services. This means that companies must provide the opportunity for people with disabilities to use services similar to those without disabilities. Whereas hearing people have access to telephones, an equivalent service for those who cannot use a telephone should be an option (e.g., a video relay service by which the Deaf can make calls in American Sign Language).

Title V contains miscellaneous other provisions, including protection of individuals who assert their rights under ADA from retaliation.

In summary, Titles I, II, and III are most relevant for postsecondary educational institutions. Titles II and III protect the rights of students with disabilities to have access to services of the University (or other educational facility).

The ADA considers the following definition of **disability**:

with respect to an individual: a physical or mental impairment that substantially limits one or more of the major life activities of such individual; a record of such an impairment; or being regarded as having such an impairment

With that comes the definition of **Major Life Activity**:

refers to activities that an average person can perform with little or no difficulty. Major life activities include, but are not limited to: caring for oneself, performing manual tasks, seeing, hearing, eating, sleeping, walking, standing, sitting, reaching, lifting, bending, speaking, breathing, learning, reading, concentrating, thinking, communicating, interacting with others, and working; and the operation of a major bodily function, including functions of the immune system, special sense organs and skin; normal cell growth; and digestive, genitourinary, bow-el, bladder, neurological, brain, respiratory, circulatory, cardiovascular, endocrine, hemic, lym-phatic, musculoskeletal, and reproductive functions. The operation of a major bodily function includes the operation of an individual organ within a body system.

Okay, so in a University (or other postsecondary) setting, to qualify for services one must have im-pairment in a major life activity. That person must also satisfy the requirements for admission to the University and (with reasonable accommodation) be able to perform the essential skills for the coursework, such as being able to understand the content of classes. Suppose that you have applied for college and been accepted. You must take responsibility for your own education. The difference between high school and college is that in high school people checked in with you, monitored your progress, and offered you accommodations. In college, you must take the responsibility to register as a student with a disability in order to receive accommodations.

Each college should have a process by which students can register or identify themselves confiden-tially as students with disabilities in need of accommodation. Identifying yourself in college as a stu-dent with a disability is optional, although it may be required if you want to request accommoda-tions. A student should have current (within the past three years) documentation of the disability. This documentation should come from a professional, possibly a doctor or psychologist. Typically, the documentation will identify and describe the disability. It may also have suggestions for accommoda-tions. While a copy of your high school IEP may be helpful for you in terms of thinking about what accommodations to request, the Disability Resources (DR) office may not accept that as a formal doc-umentation of disability, so be prepared to show diagnostic paperwork. Once documentation with the appropriate office is in order, you must be ready and able to articulate your needs for accommo-dation.

This means that you must be able to explain how your disability affects your ability to do coursework and participate in the institution's activities as well as what accommodations would make the course-work and institution accessible for you. For example, if you are blind you must explain how the DR office can make a traditional textbook accessible for you. Maybe you need textbooks Brailled or con-verted to PDFs you can access via your computer. Think carefully about all aspects of a classroom. The teacher may have PowerPoints showing in the classroom, so you may need a digital copy of those for your screenreader. Perhaps you are to be handling chemicals in a lab setting and will need assistance safely manipulating the chemicals you cannot see. Consider a different situation: you are profoundly deaf and need to take a PE class. You may need an interpreter because your classmates are spread out over a soccer field and you cannot read your teammates' lips. Perhaps you have a dancing unit and you are expected to become a competent dancer. By now, you are seeing that there are many kinds of classes, many kinds of disabilities, and many factors to consider for each course. For many people, it helps to email with or meet with the teachers of classes you need to take. This gives you the opportunity to ask about what is required of you in the class, find out how testing works, explore how content is delivered, and understand where you might need accommodation in order to successfully participate in and access all aspects of the professor's course.

Reasonable accommodation:

> *any change in the work environment [or instructional setting] or in the way things are customarily done that enables an individual with a disability to enjoy equal opportunities.*

IDEA mandates that schools provide reasonable accommodation, which gives the student access to all aspects of a course and campus. It does *not* give the student an unfair advantage in coursework. The following paragraphs list some of the reasonable accommodations this writer has seen and heard of.

There are many potential barriers to physical accessibility on a college campus, blocking access to facilities by people who use wheelchairs or scooters or cannot take stairs for other reasons. Adding a ramp into a building or changing the building a class or service is offered in may be required if there is no accessible entrance to the building. One may consider moving a class to the ground floor when the elevator is broken or there is no elevator. Students may need preferential scheduling in order to block off enough time between classes to navigate the accessible campus paths. If the school provides buses for its students, paratransit must be available for the student (such as a bus ramp or separate paratransit van).

A student may not have the motor skills to manipulate objects such as pens, calculators, or lab equipment. One accommodation could be allowing the use of a computer to take notes and turn in assignments for somebody who cannot write effectively. Students may also request note-takers or scribes. Students may request the right to audio or videotape lectures for their review. Students may request altering of the desk height if they cannot otherwise use the desk effectively. If the student has a Personal Assistant (PA) that helps them manipulate objects, that PA may be requested to assist in a lab setting.

Some accommodations are designed specifically for testing environments. These may be helpful for students with learning or neurological disabilities. These may include extended time and a distraction-free room in which the student can take the test. More frequent breaks during testing may be allowed. Some students have tests read aloud or answer aloud and have a scribe do the writing. Food may be allowed during class and testing for some students, such as those with diabetes. Requesting seating in a certain part of the room may be a reasonable accommodation for students with learning disabilities. Students may request access to speech-to-text software or text-to-speech software.

Other accommodations are often deemed appropriate for students with sensory disabilities. They may include American Sign Language (ASL) interpreters, captioning on videos shown in class or given to watch for homework, or allowing the deaf student to dance by the speaker in order to feel the vibrations. Textbooks may be Brailled or scanned onto a CD for reading by a PDF (after being cleaned up with a software called OCR). The same may be requested of any materials at the campus library: because they are available for all students, if a blind student wants to access them, they have that same right. Students may request that official University communications take place via email instead of paper if the student cannot read print. Students may need separate testing rooms if they use special equipment such as a talking calculator or scale. They may need to use magnification aids or need preferential seating in order to read lips.

Another set of accommodations relates to policy. Some course substitutions are reasonable. For example, for somebody with a math-related disability in an English program, a course substitution for algebra is reasonable. However, the course being substituted out must not be essential to the program of study. Allowing service animals in buildings is another example of a reasonable accommodation. The one exception here is if the service animal poses a threat to the healthy safety of an environment, such as a sterile room / operating room or place where food is prepared. Service animals are allowed with their handlers almost anywhere and institutional policy should reflect that.

Other accommodations may be reasonable to allow a student access to non-classroom parts of University life. Alterations may be made to dorm rooms in order to lower light switches for somebody who uses a wheelchair or to add a fire alarm flasher and doorbell for somebody who is deaf. Interpreting formal school functions, captioning sports events, buttons that open doors, providing an accessible web site and library work stations, and having wheelchair-accessible seating in the theatres and sports arenas are all ways the University should be reasonably accommodating its students with disabilities. For somebody who cannot manipulate an ID card to swipe for entry into a building, the University must provide an alternative such as a card that opens the door without a swipe or having the door watched so an assistant can help open the door.

Some accommodations are unreasonable. Accommodations that pose an undue hardship on a school may not be required. What does this mean?

Undue Burden:
> *with respect to complying with Title II or Title III of the ADA, significant difficulty or expense incurred by a covered entity, when considered in light of certain factors. These factors include: the nature and cost of the action; the overall financial resources of the site or sites involved; the number of persons employed at the site; the effect on expenses and resources; legitimate safety requirements necessary for safe operation, including crime prevention measures; or any other impact of the action on the operation of the site; the geographic separateness, and the administrative or fiscal relationship of the site or sites in question to any parent corporation or entity; if applicable, the overall financial resources of any parent corporation or entity; the overall size of the parent corporation or entity with respect to the number of its employees; the number, type, and location of its facilities; and if applicable, the type of operation or operations of any parent corporation or entity, including the composition, structure, and functions of the workforce of the parent corporation or entity.*

Consider the following unreasonable accommodation requests. What makes these requests unreasonable? What alternative accommodations can you suggest?

Jacob has a physical disability and cannot carry heavy textbooks. He asks for the school to purchase him an iPad so he can use it to view his textbooks. The school denies him the accommodation.

Jacob's request is unreasonable. The school buying him an iPad would allow him to view his textbooks for class, but there are other less costly accommodations that would do the same job. For instance, the school can put PDFs of his textbooks onto a CD he can use with a computer.

Emily is an exercise science student with dyslexia. She asks the school to waive her requirement to take physiology. The school denies this request. Then she asks to substitute an art class instead. The school denies this request too.

Since physiology is a core course requirement for the exercise science program, Emily must take it if she wants to stay in the program.

Matthew has a math disability. He has worked hard in his algebra class but is failing. He asks the school to lower the grade he needs to pass, asking essentially for a pass if he can get his grade up to 55%.

This is an unreasonable accommodation. Matthew must be held to the same standards as his peers in order to pass the course. Instead, the school refers him to the math tutoring center where he can hire a tutor that works with students in the algebra classes.

Jessica is a wheelchair mobile history student who needs to use the second floor of a library in an old building that doesn't have an elevator. She asks the school to build a ramp, knowing that it would be less costly than installing an elevator. The structure of the building would not allow for either a ramp or elevator to be installed without compromising the safety and historical integrity of the building.

While Jessica's request is thoughtful and often an accommodation used by schools, this situation is more complicated because of the building's age and structure. The school offers to help Jessica use the library system to see what books are on the second floor and then they will make sure a library assistant will bring her any books she wants to see. Since it is not possible to safely add a ramp or elevator, this alternative is acceptable.

As you are seeing, unreasonable accommodations involve the financial burden to the institution (is the school even capable of affording that accommodation?), the necessity of an accommodation when an alternative could be used just as well, accommodations that provide personal services (such as a personal care attendant or providing hearing aids), accommodations that fundamentally alter the nature of a building, service or program, or accommodations that give the student with a disability an advantage over her peers.

You will also see that when an accommodation is considered by the school to be an undue burden, there may be other alternatives. I have found it helpful to look for a compromise. If you are open to other ideas and brainstorming with the school, you will be more likely to find an acceptable alternative accommodation. Look for a situation that meets the needs of the student and the school.

Okay, so what else *can* schools opt to do for their students with disabilities?

There are many services schools can provide for their students with disabilities in order to provide a system of checks that allow these students to thrive as students. For example, Johnson County Community College provides free tutoring through their Access services.

"Access Services believes that tutoring is of great benefit to many students. Even though tutoring is not an accommodation guaranteed by the Americans with Disabilities Act, tutoring is a service that JCCC has committed to providing through various resource centers on campus. Access Services also provides tutoring to qualifying students when available."

Schools can provide environments for students to practice the conversation about accommodations with teachers. They can meet with students to help determine study schedules. Schools can also foster an environment of inclusion that welcomes diversity. Some institutions have gone as far as creating a Disability Cultural Center. The benefit of this entity (which is different from a DR office) is that a cultural center provides opportunity for social interaction and exploration, whereas a DR office is often bound by confidentiality and cannot help students socially.

I feel like one of the most helpful things a school can do is educate staff about working with people with disabilities. The more open they make this topic, the easier it is for teachers and students to engage in dialogue about how to make accommodations for a course work for the student. After all, we have the same goals: teachers want their material to be used and understood, students want the opportunity to learn, and schools want students to stay in school.

Special Notes
These notes I feel are important to the discussion on accommodations but I did not see a better place to mention them.

Schools can *not* charge an individual for accommodations.

Students are required to document a disability with the DR office if they wish to receive accommodations through the University. However, when discussing accommodations with professors, students are *not* required to name a disability. If they prefer, they may just explain the accommodation and what the accommodation helps them do. (This is similar to the situation where a store owner cannot ask what a service animal's owner's disability is but they are allowed to ask what task the animal performs (or helps perform) for the owner.

What Can Schools do that Goes Beyond the Law?
By Alec Frazier

It should be noted that in this section that I use the term disability services when referring to the office in your school that deals with accommodations.

A truly accommodating staff at an office of disability services will often do things for you that reach beyond the call of duty. There is one thing above all else that people at schools can do to go beyond the law: they can be nice to you.

For example, say you need help contacting the local transportation system in your town in order to get a disability pass. If a staff member at your disability services office makes the call on your behalf, it is much more likely for the transportation system officer in charge to make a response, from one professional to another. If you are having trouble working with a professor, a helpful disability services officer might offer to contact the professor on your behalf, or he or she might offer to provide valuable literature to the professor outlining recommended guidelines to follow in regards to a communication and/or learning style that better suits your needs.

Another important factor is that a truly helpful disability services office will be direct and honest with you. For example, texts in alternate formats sometimes take a few weeks to become available. I once attended a school that promised almost instantaneous availability for alternate format texts, but I was disheartened when it took up to six weeks for the texts I needed to become available. When I transferred to a four-year school, I mentioned this problem to my office of disability services. The person responsible said, "We're not going to lie to you; it will take a few weeks to get your materials." My response was happiness to have been told the truth up front so that I could make arrangements in the meantime.

You might find that disability service offices are filled with people you can talk to during troubling situations. Other times, you might find that disability services offices are in a rather disenfranchised position within the institute of higher learning they reside in. For example, the resources of the office department might be limited. This is where having polite, honest, active, sympathetic staff can be of the most help to students with disabilities. There is a world of difference between an office that is cold and clinical and gives off an air of doing things because it must and an office that is willing to do whatever it can (within limited resources) to go the extra mile.

For students who are on the autistic spectrum, here are some ideas where disability services office can be of help by:

- Establishing a climate of success and empowering self-advocates on the autistic spectrum to be a part of their educational plan.
- Assisting with the arrangement of weekly contact with specified professors so that students on the spectrum can check in and get information that might have been missed or misunderstood, etc.
- Providing direct access to a counselor who is familiar with students who are on the spectrum.

- Providing resources on navigating dorm life, choosing nutritious cafeteria foods, and choosing suitable college-based social activities.
- Providing resources for professors about respectful interaction that includes tips on helpful communication strategies.
- Providing information on campus-based advocacy groups geared toward students on the spectrum.
- Encouraging students on the spectrum to voice their individual needs related to education and campus life and to seek support.
- Offering note takers to assist with what has been discussed in classes.
- Providing resources to students on the spectrum on various topics that are neurodiversity-friendly and up to date.

How Students Can Cope with and Voice Their Frustrations

By Leah Jane Grantham

When I was a teenager, my favorite book series was the *Anastasia* series, by Lois Lowry, dealing with the (mis)adventures of a Boston teen, Anastasia Krupnik. I strongly identified with Anastasia's awkwardness, bossiness, book smarts, and need for self-assurance. One of my favorite books in the series was *Anastasia, Ask Your Analyst*. The ceremonial analyst in this case was a bust (sculpture) of Sigmund Freud that Anastasia picked up at a garage sale, believing that she could talk to the bust as a means of sorting through personal difficulties and frustrations. By adding a marker smile to the bust's mouth, "Sigmund", Anastasia's analyst, was born, and he proceeded to help her through some interesting and difficult problems, including a science project and stress over her relationship with her parents. Anastasia's approach is just one of the many unique ways you can approach talking about your frustrations. In this essay, I'll cover a multitude of ways of talking about and working through your frustrations—none of which involve plaster renditions of famous people, I promise.

Dealing with your frustrations can be difficult, even if you have a strong, supportive network of friends and loved ones surrounding you. I've been at two phases in my life, once when I didn't have a strong support network and once when I did. While it was infinitely more desirable to have the support network, both situations proved to have their unique challenges while I was undergoing some frustrating and difficult situations. When I was without a support network, living alone in a place where I didn't have any friends who lived close enough to come and visit me, I felt isolated and angry, because I didn't have a healthy means to communicate my frustrations with someone who could listen and respond. When I found myself a healthy and strong support network, I still withheld from talking about my frustrations because I was concerned that if I vented, I would risk losing my friends by dumping all of my problems on them. It took me a while to get comfortable enough with my friends to share my problems with them, but in the meantime, I had some methods for coping with my frustrations and building up my trust:

Building trust through listening to others. My friends and I have come a long way, and one of the ways I learned to trust them is by seeing that they too had problems and frustrations and making sure that if they needed me to listen to them and offer support, I would be available. I didn't push myself on them or try to crowd into their lives when they were going through a difficult period. I just tried to let them know, through my words, that if they wanted someone to talk to, I'd be willing to listen. I find that, in most cases, if you offer support to a friend, without letting them become dependent upon you (respect your own limits in the conversation and remember that their problems are theirs, not yours), then you can expect them to give you the same type of support in return.

An outlet without an audience. Much like how Anastasia used Sigmund, I used a paper diary and a LiveJournal blog. Blogging and writing in a diary were cathartic, because they didn't have a specific audience I had to keep in mind, so I didn't have to mince on details or censor myself in any way. When I'm speaking to another person, I tend to keep their sensibilities in mind and will usually focus more on details that they can help me with or ones that I feel are the most important. With a medium like a journal, online or print, I can "spill my guts" so to speak. Privacy settings can range from the electronic making it so that only you can read it, to the manual keeping your diary in a secret place or burning it/tearing it up after you've gotten your feelings on paper.

A cathartic activity. The problem with frustrations, for me, is that they take up a great deal of mental energy. This leads to an imbalance between my mental energy level and my physical energy level, where I feel mentally drained, but my body isn't tired enough for me to rest. To bring them more into balance and take my mind off my frustrations, at least temporarily, I pick a physically demanding activity that will give me a chance to physically work out my frustrations without using up any more mental energy. Stimming is usually my first choice, followed by running. But any physical activity that takes a great deal of physical energy will do, such as a physical contact sport, or performing a physically demanding task, like cleaning the house. After the activity, I'm both physically and mentally exhausted and I feel ready to rest. Once you're in the right mood for it, resting is excellent for putting your problems into perspective and helping you work through them.

Once you feel comfortable enough talking about your frustrations with a friend, loved one, or therapist, it's important to consider which one you'd be more comfortable with. A therapist is usually the best choice, because they are trained on how to handle frustrations in patients, usually have no personal stake in what may be causing you frustrations, are bound to confidentiality. In addition, you're paying them, so it's less likely you'll feel any guilt or anxiety about "dumping" your difficulties on them. However, therapists aren't always accessible for financial, personal, or distance reasons, and they vary in quality and effectiveness. If you have a friend or loved one you trust and can feel safe in confiding in, that's also a good option. If your frustrations are being caused by other people you both know, it is your choice whether you talk about it with them or pick someone who is more "objective" and removed from the situation.

If you find someone who is trusting, who listens to you, and who helps you through your problems, then you're quite lucky. Try to be as good of a friend to them as they are to you.

Monitoring Accessibility on Your Campus

By Allegra Stout

Monitoring your campus's accessibility can be an essential part of advocating for improvements. Initially, an accessibility assessment can show current strengths and problem areas, so that you know where to focus your efforts. As time goes on, evaluating accessibility at regular intervals can show how successful your efforts have been, as well as other improvements the college has made or new problems that have come up. This will help focus your work for change.

Gathering information about your campus's accessibility also helps increase your power to negotiate with the administration. For example, if you meet with administrators about perpetually broken automatic door openers, they are likely to take you more seriously if you can explain how long certain door openers have been broken than if you can only provide personal stories of the problem.

If you decide to monitor your campus's accessibility, a first step is to determine what types of accessibility you will consider. Access includes physical, online, social, sensory, academic, and other considerations. It is not possible to monitor every single type of accessibility, so you might start by choosing a few that are pressing issues on your campus or that you are already planning to work on.

Some types of accessibility are more easily monitored than others. For example, information about wheelchair access is often available on university websites and can be supplemented by physically checking buildings for adherence to ADA regulations. It may be more difficult to gather complete information about professors' openness to students who participate in atypical ways in class discussions, such as whether or not particular professors allow students to submit questions in writing rather than verbally during class. For types of accessibility that are harder to monitor, like professors' willingness to accommodate, there are sometimes indirect signs that can be assessed, like whether or not professors include statements about disability services in their syllabi. Keep in mind, though, that these indirect cues do not always correspond with actual accessibility.

Depending on your or your student group's relationship with your campus's ADA coordinator (a legally required administrative position), this person may be very helpful. She or he may already have data from previous assessments of the campus's accessibility, which you can use as a starting point. Alternatively, she or he may suggest types of accessibility to consider or other administrators who may be able to provide useful information. If your ADA coordinator is difficult to work with or tries to block your efforts for any reason, strive to maintain a respectful working relationship through polite and clear communication, but also seek out true allies such as sympathetic professors and administrators.

Once you have decided what types of accessibility you want to assess and how you will measure them, develop a system for gathering and tracking the data. If several people are involved in the project, a shared online tool like Google Docs might be easiest. You could even set up a Google form to be filled out for each building/class/department, to be filled out by whoever is responsible for that area.

Monitoring accessibility can be a lot of work. It can mean surveying professors, measuring ramp angles, checking websites with screen readers, and more. It's also a great opportunity to get more people involved in your group. If you set up clear and simple guidelines for how to measure particular types of accessibility, you might be able to get volunteers to take on part of the work. These individuals may become interested and join your group, but in any case, they will have learned a little about access and contributed to an important project. You might want to reach out to other students through fliers, blogs, listservs, and whatever advertising tools are common on your campus. Perhaps you could plan an "accessibility scavenger hunt," in which groups of volunteers visit different buildings with checklists of accessibility features to assess.

Of course, if you don't have the resources, time, or people to monitor several types of accessibility right now, it's fine to start with just one or two areas. As always, plan carefully with your group to make sure your project is realistic.

Once you have collected information, take the time to carefully look through it. If someone in your group has experience with statistics or graphs, it might be useful to see if that person can create some kind of report. In any case, look for problem areas, and be open to surprises. Are there problems you didn't expect? Are the problems you did expect supported by the data? Alternatively, are there notable strong points? If you see, for example, that 99% of professors include friendly statements about disability services on their syllabi, you may want to thank whoever made that happen, whether it's members of your groups, department chairs, or your faculty allies.

Presenting your accessibility survey results to administrators can help them see the scope and seriousness of problems on your campus, as well as show your group's dedication. You may want to arrange presentations with key administrators to highlight your most important results or those that are most relevant to their work. Having numbers on hand may make it easier to pressure them to commit to change.

Accessibility surveys are useful as one-time events to support current advocacy, but repeating them is a great way to show how far your campus has come or how much still needs to be done. Consider planning to monitor your campus's accessibility on a regular basis, perhaps every two years.

Regardless of whether you put your accessibility survey results to immediate use, be sure to save them in ways that will be useful to future students—not just next year or in two years, but even decades from now. Your information may someday be instrumental in showing how far the university has come in terms of accessibility (perhaps thanks to your group!) or in demonstrating just how long a particular access issue has persisted. You may want to designate someone each year to keep records in a binder and/or flash drive and to pass them on for the following year. Also consider giving copies of your results to faculty allies, the ADA coordinator, disability services providers, and even the university's archivists (who can often be contacted through library websites), so that your findings have a higher chance of remaining available to future generation of students. This will ensure that your hard work is as useful as possible.

Navigating Mental Health Services on Your Campus

By Emily Kronenberger

Introduction: Getting Started

Welcome to college! By continuing your education, you are on your way to building a more rewarding, independent, and stable future and you should be proud. Also, you should be aware that students today are wading through both new and familiar emotional, physical, and psychological challenges to their health, including stress and anxiety about education costs, social and interpersonal obstacles, steep competition for opportunities, difficulties in establishing balance, soaring debt, and high expectations despite a tough job market. As young people continue to juggle more demands on their time, attention, and abilities, colleges and universities are responding to a sharp increase in student demands for mental health services, from the freshman new to college life to the experienced graduate level student.

Although college students from every type of background face a range of mental health issues on today's campuses, services are being expanded to meet the needs of these students in greater numbers. As a result, some who may not have considered attending colleges or universities, studying full-time, commuting far distances, or living away from home in the past are realizing greater independence with the help of self-advocacy and better support services. This chapter will provide information and resources for navigating some of these mental health issues and accessing appropriate services on campus. We hope that you find these tools helpful as you begin your journey towards getting what you need to feel more mentally healthy and well, while reaching your academic goals. Please note that this chapter is not intended to provide legal advice and serves only as a resource guide. While you will come across some resources in the text, be sure to check out the last page of the chapter for a greater list of resource links.

If you are coming to campus with pre-existing mental health conditions, feelings of being overwhelmed, helplessness, or distress may be intensified by challenges to managing your condition in a new place or by the transition to college life. You might need to establish relationships with new health providers, or seek other trusted peers, friends, and professionals who you can add to your circle of support. Whether you have experienced mental health issues in the past or feel like you may be dealing with stress, anxiety, depression, or other issues for the first time, some good guidelines for staying healthy while managing mental health conditions include:

> **Being active** – Physical activity does not have to be strenuous and can be any movements that you are comfortable with and meet your individual needs, especially if you have physical limitations, including seated yoga poses and light stretching.

> **Eating and sleeping for mental health** – Proper nutrition and good sleep practices can improve mood, fight depression, and help you maintain focus in addition to setting the stage for better overall health.

> **Having some fun** – Remember to maintain balance by scheduling in time for you and dedicating part of your schedule to activities that you enjoy for regular breaks and fun!

> **Sticking with it** – If you were under the care of a health professional before arriving on cam-

pus, keep going with any treatments you may have started and be sure to continue with medications as instructed.

Taking the First Step: Recognizing Changes

How do you know that you may need to seek help? Sometimes we notice changes in our mood or emotions, such as feelings of deep sadness, depression, or lower self worth that may be symptoms of an emerging mental health issue.

Other emotional or behavioral changes that may signal a problem include:

- Crying more often than usual, mood swings, or lack of energy
- Feeling restless or urges to fidget
- Having defeating thoughts like, "I never wanted this," or "It's hopeless, why try?"
- Experiencing anxiety, guilt, or lots of worry
- Changes in your school performance such as suffering grades
- Feeling confused by everyday tasks or decisions
- Trouble with speaking, remembering, or thinking clearly
- More difficulty with concentration and staying focused
- Taking risks or acting in unsafe ways
- Drinking alcohol or using drugs to cope with daily life
- Frequent anger, frustration, and irritation
- Withdrawing or "shutting down" from family, friends, or social activities
- Less ability to function
- Having thoughts about hurting oneself or suicide

Let's take a moment to pause here for an important note: if at any time you have thoughts of suicide or harming yourself, please get help immediately. Go to your school health center or call the National Suicide Prevention Lifeline atl-800-273-8255 (TALK).

We might also experience physical changes that could indicate a shift in our mental health and wellness, including:

- Changes in appetite (eating too much or too little)
- Anxious or "jittery" movements
- Tension or spasm in your muscles
- Chronic pain such as joint aches or headaches
- Problems with digestion
- Changes in your sleep habits (sleeping too much or too little)
- Being unable to sleep
- Exhaustion or being tired all the time
- Cutting yourself or self-injuring in some other way

Knowing You're Not Alone

Many factors can contribute to stress and other mental health issues that impact us across our lifespan, and college is one of the most demanding periods as we grow into who we are as adults and learn to balance our responsibilities and challenges. Please know that you are not alone in these experiences. In 2010, the National College Health Survey showed that 27.3% of students identified stress as a top factor that affected their academic performance, while 18.5% identified anxiety, and 11.9% identified depression as top factors that interfered with their academic performance. The same survey found that among college students, 38.5% of men and 42.3% of women had been diagnosed with depression in the previous year.

Past trauma and toxic stresses or new routines, people, surroundings, and social situations, along with more demanding school work, worries over money, and making tough choices can influence our mental health status. In addition, relationships (even healthy and satisfying ones) can take a heavy toll upon our mental health. If you find yourself in a harmful situation, notice symptoms in more frequency or intensity than usual, or are experiencing a combination of them and you are concerned, don't ignore your feelings. If you think you are in an unhealthy relationship with a friend or intimate partner, especially one in which you have experienced verbal, physical, or sexual abuse, seek help right away. Get started by recognizing that you need care and then reach out to a trusted source so that you can feel better and be safe. It is important to remember that getting help is a healthy, positive step to take toward healing even though it may often be very difficult for many of us.

Finding Help

On your way to getting the care you need, you may feel overwhelmed about knowing who to talk to, or where to go. If you experience this, it can help to first share your thoughts with someone you trust and with whom you feel comfortable, such as a friend, teammate, parent, other family member, faith or clergy person, Resident Advisor, or a trusted professor or staff member at your school. Often, people close to you have been in similar situations and will work with you to get started in accessing help from a medical or mental health professional. If you have a circle of support or members of a social group that you can count on at home or at school, you might reach out to one of these folks and let them know you are having difficulty and seeking help.

When you are ready, your school may be the first or next stop for getting professional help. Most colleges and universities have some kind of mental health or counseling services available in their health clinics or centers, and many institutions have a whole range of mental health programs including couples counseling, support groups, meditation classes, and safe spaces for students. Over the past several years, college health systems have created services to address many mental health issues among students, including anxiety disorders, eating concerns, depression, substance abuse, and many others. In addition, schools often have helpful resources, supports, and programs that students dealing with mental health problems are unaware of, such as flexible options to continue schoolwork while receiving treatment for a mental health problem, transportation services, etc. It is especially important to find out what your school offers especially if you already have a documented disability so that they can set up appropriate supports or accommodations to help you. To find a list of your school's services, you can also use ULifeline's online referral service and get information on what is available by

visiting the link below and entering your school's name:
www.ulifeline.org/self_evaluator.

If you need help navigating services on campus, there are usually staff members who can assist with this too, including administrators in an Office of Disability Services, a Student Health Center, or a Student Services Office. Many colleges and universities have peer educators or health advisors who are trained to work with their fellow students on accessing services and can help you to find the care you need on campus. To find a certified peer educator at your school or to contact a regional peer advisor in your community, check out the BACCHUS Network's website here, www.bacchusnetwork.org/area-directory.html, or find your local Active Minds Chapter here at www.activeminds.org.

If you wish or need to seek mental health care off-campus, there are many good places to start in order to locate community resources. Check out the national services locator tool at the Substance Abuse and Mental Health Services Administration and enter your zip code for a list of nearby providers at http://store.samhsa.gov/mhlocator. If you attend a commuter, vocational or technical school or you are enrolled at a community college that does not have on-site services available, talk with your Student Support Office or a Disability Coordinator, as they might be able to refer you to a provider in the community or other resources. Get in touch with your local mental health advocacy organizations, such as a National Alliance on Mental Illness (NAMI) chapter by visiting www.nami.org.

Becoming Your Own Advocate

When you contact your college health or counseling center, let them know if you feel that your situation is an emergency. Schools may have 24-hour crisis services that can assist you, or the staff member that you speak with will tell you where to go for immediate help. If you are not in crisis, but feel you need to speak with someone soon and no-walk in services are available, do not get discouraged. Make and keep your appointment, and if there is a long wait time, ask to be placed on a cancellation list and be notified if anything opens up. Following up is important too, so if you make an initial appointment and feel that you cannot wait that long, or other issues arise after you have made your appointment, get back in touch with the health center or provider and ask to speak with an office manager, nurse, or leave a message for a therapist to call you back so that you can explain your situation and get help.

Be sure to find out what costs you are responsible for when seeking care on campus or off-campus in the community. For example, whether you are covered under a university health plan, under your parents' health insurance, or by a public insurance plan, it is important to find out where your insurance is accepted, if there are co-pays, tests, or other costs that you will be responsible to pay, and what financial assistance may be available to you either through school or community assistance programs.

Many students express concerns over privacy issues when seeking mental health care, especially if they are covered under their parents' health insurance. Students are entitled to their right to privacy of medical and mental health care information under federal laws, with some exceptions, such as if a health provider feels that a student is a danger to themselves or someone else. To get complete information on your rights to privacy, reasonable accommodations, and actions you can take if you feel that you have been discriminated against or that these rights or other civil rights have been violated, visit the Bazelon Center for Mental Health Law's website at http://www.bazelon.org/. The Leadership 21 Committee, a group of young mental health rights activists at Bazelon, has put together a comprehensive campus mental health rights guide, called Know Your Rights, which is available here:

http://www.bazelon.org/Portals/0/pdf/YourMind-YourRights.pdf

Helping Friends

If you notice symptoms or situations mentioned in the beginning of this chapter among one of your friends or peers, and you are concerned for their health or safety, please don't ignore this either. Talk with them about what you have observed or may be going on, and then try to see if they are willing to get help. Offer to go with them if they are anxious. If you don't feel comfortable or know what to say right away, you can talk with a crisis worker at the National Suicide Prevention Lifeline, ask questions, and get some guidance on how to start the conversation by calling 1-800-273-TALK.

The Bottom Line

Letting mental health conditions go untreated is like neglecting any other ache, pain, or part of your body in need of care and can lead to unpleasant and dangerous outcomes, both in the short and long-term, for your health. Help is available, and aside from getting the best care quickly in order to start the healing process, there may be other significant benefits to beginning treatment at this point in your young adult life. Each of us deserves the opportunity to live an independent, enjoyable, and full life based on our individual desires and dreams, so don't delay in getting the help you need!

Managing Mental Hygiene: The Care & Keeping of Your Mind
By Leah Jane Grantham

What do self-care and mental hygiene mean to you? Are you even familiar with these terms? If you are, you can count yourself among the fortunate. Many don't realize that they exist, and that they're essential components towards a happy, healthy existence. Do you brush your teeth every day? Do you floss? Soap yourself up in the shower? Wash your hair? Shave? All of these things are considered part of a regular body-care routine, and it's considered, at least, to be rude not to do so, lest people have to deal with the side-effects of your neglecting your bodily hygiene, such as the odours associated with bad breath and bodily odours like sweat. Neglecting mental hygiene can have a similar negative impact on yourself and your interactions with others and is equally important, but strangely neglected in many conversations about health.

I have always been deeply devoted to my physical self-care and had a book when I was a pre-teen, directed towards young girls going through puberty, called *The Care & Keeping of You*, which pressed the importance of physical hygiene upon me with vivid similes, such as, "food caught between your teeth can rot and stink just like garbage". I believe that, like food in between your teeth, bad thoughts, stress, anxiety, and unaddressed issues can get caught in the (metaphorical) folds of your brain and can fester there, impacting your interpersonal relationships, work, school, and overall happiness. But if you take an effort to floss out what's stuck there, and clean your mind with self-care rituals on a regular basis, even moments of great distress can become manageable.

It can be difficult to write a general piece about mental self-care and managing mental hygiene, because there's no standard process for doing it. In *The Care & Keeping of You*, there were lessons on how to shave, how to properly brush your teeth, and ways of washing your face. But people all have different hobbies, different concerns, and different stress relievers in their lives; you can't generalize as heavily as you can by presuming that everyone uses a toothbrush. As an autistic individual, I've found that I have means of self-care that range from being quite common to those which cause people to cock eyebrows when I describe them. But there's no more or less valid way to practice self-care and perform mental hygiene checks; there's only what works best for you and your needs. With that said, I'm going to share a few of my own mental hygiene/self-care rituals, not because I think that they are the best or only way of managing your mental hygiene, but because they can give you an idea of what kind of activities are a good starting point for figuring out what works best for you in your mental hygiene routine:

> **Internet Retail Therapy:** Real brick-and-mortar stores are often a hit-and-miss experience for me, as someone on the autism spectrum. Pushy salespeople, bright lights, and lacklustre selection for people with special sensory considerations can often make shopping for clothes and other products be downright unpleasant or inaccessible for me. The only stores I genuinely enjoy browsing in regularly are bookstores, and I consider browsing a bookstore or a library to be a mental hygiene ritual in and of itself. But for most situations, when I'm stressed out and want to unwind, I get great pleasure in online shopping, even if I don't buy anything. Putting beautiful clothes, accessories, and art onto my Pinterest Boards, Etsy Favourites, or Amazon Wish List is enough satisfaction, most of the time, and I can conjure them up for purchase later, should I need a stronger sort of therapy. Once in a while, just as a self-soothing

mechanism, I'll go through my various online wish lists and rearrange the items, according to how badly I want them. If I do buy something, I try to keep it small, like buying a single song, a pretty new shade of lipstick, or a video game I've been meaning to play for ages.

Stimming: If you're not familiar with this term, it's basically short for "self stimulation" and can mean a variety of things, from flapping your hands to rocking your head to pacing. Stimming is a lot like general self-soothing and self-care, in that there's no "proper" way to do it, but one can almost always recognize it for what it is.

Personally, I stim by flapping my hands, rocking back in forth in rhythm to music from my iPod, spinning in chairs and on swing sets, rubbing my face against a piece of soft fabric like fur or silk, rolling around on soft surfaces like rugs and blankets, humming, singing, and brushing my hair vigorously. You may have been doing stimming all of your life without realizing that it was stimming. If you want to try to experiment with new ways to stim, or try to figure out which way is right for you, try using an object as the centre of your stimming (aka a stim toy) such as a stuffed animal, a comfortable blanket, a piece of fabric with a pleasing texture, or a soft, squishy toy. After a good session of stimming, I'm both physically and mentally relaxed and feel much better about just about everything in the world.

Beauty Rituals: A lot of people find this particular method of self-care to be unusual, but I can personally attest to the difference taking about an hour to care for your appearance can make to your mood. When I am having a bad day, or I feel particularly down, I set aside about an hour of my day and take a bath, pamper myself, and put on an outfit that's comfortable and attractive. When I look in the mirror, I can smile to myself and say "Wow, I'm fabulous!" and feel much better. Whatever it is you do to make yourself feel good looking and fabulous, whether that's having an extra-long bath, trying out a new make-up product, or getting a haircut, it can do a great deal for your mental hygiene.

Cooking: In my case, cooking is a type of multipurpose therapy. Cooking for other people allows me to express how much I care for them by putting love and effort into the food I make for them. I'm currently using traditional recipes connected to my heritage as a way of getting in touch with my roots and learning about my ancestry. I also use it as a means of relaxing; my strong sense of smell makes a kitchen where delicious things are cooking a warm and welcoming place, the very best kind of aromatherapy. And finally, putting effort into the food I make helps keep me from engaging in a formerly harmful habit of mine emotional eating.

Exercise: After one recent stressful event in my life, I went to the library and picked up a copy of Haruki Murakami's *What I Talk About When I Talk About Running* and began working on becoming a runner. I'm a work in progress. I speedwalk about once a day and try to run in short, 5 minute bursts. While I'm running, I don't have to focus on anything but the speed of my feet against the pavement, the rhythm of the music in my ears, and the pleasant burn of being warmed by exercise. Any exercise, within your abilities and enjoyment, can serve the same function that running does for me.

I want to make it clear that practicing mental hygiene and self-care is not a magic cure-all for stress, nor is it the ultimate key to managing your mental health, any more than brushing your teeth means you never have to go to the dentist or eating well means you don't ever need to get your blood pressure or cholesterol checked. Mental hygiene is a small part of a larger self-care routine that involves doing what you feel it takes to keep yourself feeling 'alright'. That can include therapy, medication, or whatever else you feel you need. Mental hygiene is just one of many tools in your self-care repertoire, and how you do it is entirely up to you.

Identifying Non-Traditional Accommodations

By Leah Jane Grantham

Non-disabled people are sometimes surprised by the accommodations disabled people require. Even in places where disabled people have strong legal protections that enshrine their rights to accommodation, they may still find themselves in situations where they need to create their own accommodations. Thank goodness disabled people can often find accommodations in the most unlikely of places.

I've found myself in many situations where I needed to work on non-traditional accommodations, either by myself, or with the help of a dedicated and supportive advocate. Non-traditional accommodations can face scrutiny and gate-keeping measures from more "official"-minded people in the medical and disability community, but you have to remember that what matters is what works for you personally and what you feel works best for you. Only you can decide that, not your doctor, advocate, caretakers, or therapist.

I'm a university student, so my non-traditional accommodations have mostly focused on ways that I can equally participate with my classmates in the many learning situations I am faced with. Since I have sensory processing disorder, and I have difficulty hearing out of my left ear, I always try to talk to the professor in my class about arranging for me to have a spot near the front, and to their left, so that I can hear them with my right ear and have minimal distraction. This is a relatively easy accommodation to make, with almost no fuss once I explain my reasons.

A more difficult to attain non-traditional accommodation has been an iPad. I'm (mostly) verbal and articulate, so when I have requested an iPad in the past to help me organize my daily life, I have faced resistance, because it was presumed that since I wasn't using it for its commonly accepted use in accommodation—namely, nonverbal communication—that I didn't really need it. But if I did have an iPad, I wouldn't have to worry about losing important paperwork because it would all be stored on it, and I could set reminders for myself to eat, shower, meet people, and do other daily tasks that often get lost in the chaos of my mind. I could also store everything I need in a single unit and not aggravate my long history of back problems with a heavy bag. For now, I'm using a variety of substitutes in order to maintain my executive functioning and day-to-day schedule, such as an alarm clock, note-cards, and reminders written on sticky notes, but I'm hoping to get an iPad soon, with the help of an advocate.

By using products that are not meant at all to have an accommodation purpose, and by creating your own accommodations from scratch, you can go even further in getting creative with your accommodations.

Among these different and new accommodations, I've done things like opt to keep a patch of fur in my pocket for calming myself down during stressful moments. I also alter all of my clothes so that there are no tags or itchy linings in them. I keep earplugs in my pockets at all times in case of a noisy environment, and I take a series of "mini-breaks" at work so that I can stim in private and then be at the top of my productivity after a session. Everybody has different ways to go about accommodations, but the important thing is to explain to those who you are dealing with that accommodations make it possible for you to be a healthy, positive, productive worker, student, and person—which is what everybody wants, right?

In my life, the most difficult part with non-traditional accommodations has been explaining their purposes. To counter this, I often print note-cards to explain the purpose of my accommodations. Here's an example:

> *Hello, if you are receiving this card, chances are you asked me why I'm doing (insert your accommodation here). I'm glad you asked. This is my way of ensuring that I am at the top of my mental and physical health, by accommodating my own needs and making myself as comfortable as possible. It may seem unusual, but this is what works for me, and I wouldn't have it any other way. If you have any non-invasive, respectful questions for me, I'll try to answer them to the best of my abilities. Thank you for your interest!*

I have different methods and ideas for creating my own accommodations, but I think that the greatest accommodation that I've ever come across wasn't even my own idea, and wasn't autism or even disability-specific. It was a safer spaces policy.

What is a safer spaces policy? Well, the way it's executed differs, but at the core, the idea is to establish a comfortable, enjoyable environment where everybody participating feels safe, welcomed, and happy. It's considered the responsibility of everybody in the room, not just people in positions of power or management, to maintain this space. At my workplace, our safer spaces policy boiled down to three simple rules of conduct: respect the boundaries of others, respect your own boundaries, and assume positive intent.

I would like to talk the most about number two when it comes to how safer spaces intersect with accommodations. Respecting your own boundaries means that you don't over-exert yourself or try to put "too much on your plate", and that if you have a particular need, you take care of it immediately, and prioritize your health and needs over work or other duties. For example, if there's an intense discussion going on, or if the lighting is making me uncomfortable, or if I need to take a few moments to stim, relax, grab a drink of water or use the bathroom, I'm free to do so without being criticized for it, which is what has happened at other workplaces. It also means that no matter what is making me uncomfortable, I have the right to speak out against it and have it stopped. Since everybody in a safer space is accountable to each other, rather than being accountable to an authority figure, like a boss, it's easier to call attention to a person whose behavior is making you uncomfortable.

You don't have to introduce a safer spaces policy to your workplace to make it effective as an accommodation tool. You can simply talk about the principles of it to your boss/coworkers/ professors, and see if they respond well to it. If they do, then you can do a "trial" run where you try to live by those principles, and see if they improve the environment and make it easier to deal with moments when you need "down time", or when you need to set boundaries around or stop an undesirable behavior in the workplace.

The reason I'm particularly fond of thinking of a safer spaces policy as an accommodation is because too many stories about disability are framed through a lens of changing a disabled person in order to fit into the environment of a workplace, university, or other locations. I believe that the true focus of accommodations in all circumstances should be to adapt the environment to fit the needs of everybody, disabled people included. But, until the rest of the world catches up to how much simpler and more effective that is, oftentimes the onus will be on disabled people to create their own accommodations and to justify them, especially if they seem different or unconventional. So don't be afraid to go forward with nontraditional accommodations, because at the end of the day, it's your creativity that's up against an ableist society, and you are winning by creating your own accommodations. Consider it a sweet victory, and good luck!

Disability Services on Campus: Common Issues and Challenges

By Alec Frazier

It should be noted that in this section I use the term disability services when referring to the office in your school which deals with accommodations.

Just as a student with disabilities may be the victim of discrimination on campus, an office of disability services may be the victim of institutional discrimination. Disability services offices are generally given fewer funds, less space, less resources, and overall less of a voice in the affairs of the school. This may be more or less readily apparent depending on whether you go to a state school or a private institution. This is also not to say that the administration of your school has it out for people with disabilities. Rather, this is because disability services still has a relatively new and less well established position in many schools.

The next time you go to your office of disability services, take a look at exactly where it is situated and how it is laid out. Does it have its own building? If so, is that building in a place where it is easily accessible to people with disabilities and the student body at large? If it does not have its own building, is it part of a larger learning center, or does it have independent offices? Are those offices small or large?

If you are able to answer these questions, you will learn a lot about the university's potential view on its office of disability services. For example, the amount of space an office has in a school is generally relevant to the amount of priority it is given. Sadly, it is often not enough.

Let's say your office of disability services has its own building, but it is not accessible for individuals who use wheelchairs. It is important to ring up this matter to the office by mentioning it to a counselor, or by sending a message voicing your concern to the office Director via email—or you might prefer to drop off a note to be delivered in the Director's message box if you prefer.

The main point here is to feel free to bring up accessibility issues with a disability services office. Another example would be if the quiet study room provided for students with disabilities happens to be too loud (if your college even offers such a room). What you could do in this situation is notify the person at the front desk and request help. Maybe there is not yet a rule in the study room in regards to scented perfumes and other such products. Some students have sensory sensitivities that would make the study room provided inaccessible if fragrances are detected. Again, this is something you should feel empowered to mention to the office. Oftentimes, solutions to such problems can be as cheap and easy as making a new rule and a new sign stating it. You might even offer to help if you have a good idea or the skills to remedy the situation.

<u>Questions to Ask Disability Services</u>
By Alec Frazier

Students (or prospective students) often contact an office of disability services for specific reasons. For example, a student knows he or she has a certifiable disability and that necessary accommodations are warranted. Another reason for a student to contact the office might be that they suspect they might have a certifiable disability or condition that warrants accommodations. Another student might contact the office because they feel overwhelmed by coursework and need help with managing the load. Another common scenario is that a student might feel that making the office of disability services aware of their disability may open up opportunities to them that would otherwise not exist.

It often helps to generate a list of questions you wish to ask your office of disability services before meeting for the first time. Sample questions include, but are certainly not limited to:

- What services can you provide me?
- What is the communication structure of your office of disability services? Specifically, to whom should I speak if I need help or have a question? When and how do I contact this person?
- Do you honor the accommodations recommended in my existing IEP, or do you require the creation of a new one?
- I have trouble with _____. Can you help accommodate me with that?
- Are professors and other staff aware of disability regulations on campus?
- What efforts does the school make to prevent, resolve, and protect students with disabilities from acts of prejudice, hate or threats of harm? To whom do I report such behaviors?
- I have a mobility issue and/or trouble getting from place to place. Do you have paratransit available?
- Are there assistive technologies that can help me, and if so can you provide me with a copy?
- How long does this process take?
- Do you have a good working relationship with the residence hall staff?
- What kind of disability related peer support is available to me? Ex: organizations, programs, locations, events, social communities.
- I have need for regular talk therapy. Is there an office on campus that can help me with that?
- I take prescription medications. Does the university health center have a pharmacy, and if so, could you put me in touch?
- How much or how little would you advise me to disclose about my disabilities, and to whom?

Some common issues for students on the autistic spectrum include, but are not limited to:

- Difficulties with juggling different priorities from managing college life to coursework to extracurricular activities to roommates and other obligations
- Sensitivities to noise and/or specific fragrances or odors
- Difficulties with finding quiet places to study or to take exams
- Managing food allergies and similar sensitivities
- Managing mental health and locating appropriate help and resources

- Dealing with bullies and/or insensitive or uneducated professors and staff
- Dealing with feelings of isolation, loneliness, and/or homesickness

Ideas for dealing with the above issues include contacting the disability services office and making an appointment to talk to someone. Another idea is to look for ideas and tips that might address your issues by searching the Internet. Also, look for advocacy groups run by students on the autism spectrum and make it a point to attend a meeting. Surely someone else on the spectrum might be having the same issues. Perhaps they might have an idea or a helpful resource. Public libraries are another avenue. For example, if you experience difficulty with being assertive about your needs, perhaps you can find a book that can coach you and provide you with some useful tips. Whatever you do, don't give up! You've come too far to let fear keep you from your dreams!

Engaging with Administration

Who Is Who? Figuring out Who You Need to Contact

By Elizabeth Boresow

The size of your University can help or hinder your progress in figuring out who you need to make contact with as a student group. When you begin to make contacts with others as a student organization, start a list of contacts. Make sure you have the following information from your contact: their first and last name, their title (Dr. or Mrs. or Ms. ...), their job title and department, their phone number, email, and office location (building and room number). This list will be an important resource for you. Try to keep it updated when administration change positions.

One of the most important things you can do is make connections with a variety of people across campus. In order to be effective as a network, it may be necessary to disclose your disability. For example, when I was explaining how my disability affected me in the classroom to one of my teachers, he disclosed a disability and told me he welcomed questions and would be willing to help put me in touch with resources on campus. Staying in touch with people who have disabilities is useful. Disabilities are pervasive in society: you will find faculty, staff and students with disabilities. Contact with these people will help you as a disability-related group to be aware of the variety of barriers there are to accessibility on your campus. Chances are these people will represent a variety of differences. Use each other's strengths and connections within disability communities to stay informed in the field. This will open doors with disability-specific larger organizations. For example, you may find a staff member who works in one of the campus buildings who is a member of the National Federation of the Blind. You may find a Graduate Teaching Assistant who has a friend at the Department of Justice, which could be helpful if you had questions about the ADA.

Privacy laws make it hard for students with disabilities to connect, especially students with hidden disabilities. One thing I always do is let my Disability Resources advisor know that I am comfortable being a resource for other students with disabilities or speaking to classes about disability. This opens the door for my advisor to contact me if a situation arises where a student is requesting a mentor or a teacher is requesting a speaker. My advisor can say that someone is looking for contact and I can give her permission to forward them my contact information.

Generally speaking, you should know your ADA Coordinator and the staff in the Disability Resources office (which could be called an Accommodations office or Accessibility Services office or something else). It is often helpful to establish a contact in departments you will communicate with often about accessibility, such as Facilities/Operations, Housing, Dining Services, Parking, and the Libraries. Human Resources and the Diversity Office (Multicultural Resource Center or Women's Center) are also good contacts to establish. In terms of other student groups, having a contact on Student Senate can be helpful. Working with the Veterans group on campus can be good, because so many veterans come back with newly acquired disabilities and try to do college.

If you can establish a good professional relationship with these contacts, they will be more likely to support your group. Take the time to learn about some of these people and develop rapport with them. Your University's web site may have their biographies and a description of their jobs and/or current research or projects as members of academia. The more people you have this contact with, the smaller your University will seem because your contacts will be able to point you in the right direction.

Networking with Faculty/Professionals

By Mike Liu

> *For this chapter, I shall refer to all networking with faculty/professionals in their respective fields as "professionals." This could refer to people you meet who are part of your university or those you meet through outside organizations; the same principles apply to whether they themselves are or are not disabled.*

Meeting a professional who can support your advocacy group on campus

A useful way to get involved in disability advocacy on a college campus is to network with professionals already involved in disability-related advocacy and/or research that both helps and uplifts the disability community you're involved with. As an autistic individual, I have been fortunate throughout my college and medical school career to have easy access to people who were able to help get a student group get started. These individuals have either worked in the autism field or knew of people on the autism spectrum from their personal or professional relationships. Also, you can learn a lot from people like this about the direction the disability research and service provision fields are moving. In return, you may be able to offer them insights into aspects they may not even have thought about.

A good way to meet with professionals is to attend classes, lectures, or symposia by the individuals you're interested in meeting. Research the topics they'll be talking about and ask insightful questions when the audience is invited to do so (I usually limit myself to two questions at most during the presentation so as to give other people a chance to ask questions too). You might also want to visit specialized departmental networking events or open houses.

Sometimes I have problems with ambient noise or I wish to engage in a little bit longer of a conversation. In that case, I usually ask the person of interest if they would care to move to a slightly quieter corner after I've introduced myself and requested a few minutes to chat. It's generally a good rule of thumb to offer others a chance to talk before taking a turn, especially if you want to cover more than one topic. For people who do not communicate via spoken correspondence, perhaps a brief note might help in introducing who you are. Be sure to mention why your preferred method of communication suits you best; it could be because you have sensory filtering issues, etc.

If you have to "cold call" (contact a person for the first time without attending a previously scheduled event) a professional, e-mail is usually a good method. One or two e-mails per week is usually plenty, as professionals tend to have extremely busy schedules with teaching, seminars, research, journal clubs, etc. Mention something very specific in terms of the papers they write or the talks they give that you are interested in. Doing so shows them you've done your research, and they might be more likely to respond. If you do not receive a response after about 2 weeks, follow-up through either with people who know them such as their professional colleagues in a class or that person's administrative assistant (only when applicable). If you hear about a professional through someone who works with or knows the professional in a significant capacity, utilize that person as your primary contact initially.

In whatever way you would like to get into contact with professionals, the basics of your introductions should indicate you are interested in starting a disability group and that you would like their involvement in increasing interest in disability advocacy. If they agree to meet with you, you're in luck! If their office is in a location that is inaccessible (e.g. an older building that may not be ADA compliant) and you know of it, suggest another location that is mutually accessible (and the accessibility issue may give the both of you something to talk about). If a professional clearly indicate that they are not interested, quickly move on to other people who may actually have an interest.

I have found that it works best for me when I keep in mind that a professional's time is often limited and so I need to make the most of my meetings with them. Be ready to explain what benefit to them it would be to support your group. Think about what a person in a given field would be interested in achieving when working with your group, and then tailor your involvement "pitch" (your persuasive discussion) as necessary.

When talking about how your group or project will improve the condition of people with disabilities, for example, a pen-pal program or an on-campus support group, let your professional contact know it will add an extra dimension to a university's community service center. When I started an advocacy group, it certainly helped that a key leadership member of my school's community service center had autistic relatives.

Whether you're creating a support group for similarly disabled individuals or gathering individuals and allies to address campus accessibility issues (for both physical and mental disabilities, although some disabilities could be a mix of both components), the point is to be able to show that involvement with your group is a valuable investment of the professional's time and that it will likely yield good returns for their career or personal motivations.

Disclosure

As for disclosure of your own condition as a motivation for starting an organization or disability cultural center, some people might not be familiar with how a disability might affect a person's goals. For example, sometimes people assume they know a person's needs because they see that they are using a wheelchair or that they are wearing hearing aids. Or perhaps someone might assume they know a person's needs just because they have learned that person is autistic ("Oh, I bet he learns visually like Temple Grandin.")

It is important for people to understand that disabilities, whether visible/invisible, can change from day to day and moment to moment. Therefore, some people might be tempted to ask how you came to be disabled out of curiosity or how you manage daily living tasks. While I certainly believe everybody is entitled to their own sense of intellectual curiosity, you have the right to set boundaries as to what details about your life you wish to disclose. Some of us want to avoid becoming what Jim Sinclair would call a "self-narrating zoo exhibit." If a person you're meeting with is only interested in that to the exclusion of all else, and they press on with deeply personal questions after you have asked them to stop, get out of that interaction *immediately*. Let the person know that you respect their time but that what they can offer is not what you're looking for. To avoid being a "case-study," as opposed to a sentient person, avoid forming connections with such people. After all, you're most likely looking for a person interested in becoming an effective ally to your disability advocacy group.

If you don't choose to disclose your specific disability immediately, utilize your own research from scientific/professional journals or other research to illustrate a demonstrative need in a particular disability community. Let your idea speak for itself. Generally, people might take that as it is without too many personal questions as long as you seem to be honest and sincere.

If a professional has specifically been involved in a particular disability field for many years, chances are they will likely recognize your specific characteristics as related to the disability your group will support. When I first met with my research mentor at the autism neuroimaging lab I worked in during college, I did not initially reveal that I was autistic. Yet he was able to recognize the autistic side of me almost immediately from factors like my gaze, my prosody, and my elocutions because he is a physician and has been trained to recognize the autistic patterns in the patients he sees. I came to know this because when I asked him for a letter of recommendation to medical school, he mentioned to me that he would foresee me having difficulties "with the art side of medicine." Additionally, he had asked me about my language skills and my social skills, and he even asked if I have any repetitive behaviors. I had no idea how "repetitive behaviors" fit into the scheme of being good doctor, but it tipped me off that he knew something extra about myself that I had not initially revealed.

He mentioned that I should think of a career in medicine that does not involve a lot of interaction with people such as pathology or radiology primarily because of some of my personal social difficulties. I do acknowledge that these fields are important in many ways. I know my mentor meant well, but I was admittedly slightly hurt by his reservations about my ability to interact with and advocate for patients on the autism spectrum directly (which is the whole point of why I wanted to go into medicine as a career). In the end, I understood that he meant that while he didn't think that I could not become a good clinical physician, there were many challenges associated with the autism spectrum. I needed to have a clear understanding in pursuing such a career. Overall, I felt my mentor's intentions were more cautious than openly antagonistic.

On the other hand, some faculty may not acknowledge your condition freely. Professionals who have for the most part seen certain kinds of individuals with disabilities may not be able to recognize more subtle manifestations. Some faculty members I've met never acknowledged my autism spectrum diagnosis when I spoke with them. Most likely it was something about my overall profile: an Asian-American student who seems to have no self-care difficulties, was mainstream schooled his entire life, graduated from high school with an International Baccalaureate diploma, graduated from Johns Hopkins Univeristy with a B.S. and M.A. in Biology with honors, and rarely if ever stimmed in public.

In my experience many professionals might extend an invitation to help you network to get a disability assessment (often necessary to get college accommodations, especially in the case of learning disabilities). For me, my mentor managed to help me find a study to get me potentially "officially diagnosed," and he even offered his professional opinion when he met my parents to discuss my condition.

Keep in mind the kind of organization the professional may be working for when you network with them, especially if the organization is not affiliated with your institute of higher learning. Be sure to research organizations thoroughly via their websites. If they are non-profit organizations registered with the IRS, they most likely will have financial forms available to the public. Observe how they portray individuals with disabilities and the involvement of such individuals in the group's leadership.

If it is an organization that relies on pity and fear mongering to raise money, steer clear of becoming involved with such a group. On the other hand, if a group genuinely seems interested in offering constructive quality-of-life services to individuals with disabilities and empowering them, even if you do not agree with their methods completely, then this might be good group to initiate a dialogue with to help improve disabilities supports.

Relationships with Professionals

What professionals can learn from you and vice versa is the crux of the relationship and your opportunity to talk about self-advocacy in autism or any other disability. When introducing the concept of disability rights, create common ground. You could do this, for example, by stating how accommodating different learning styles allows students to utilize hidden creative gifts that benefit academia. Mention how creating better alternative and augmentative communication (AAC), devices (such as computers in a pen-pal program) could open new social avenues. There are many other potential projects you could undertake, like creating technological apps for various disabilities if you're a Computer Science major or tackling cultural barriers to understanding disability if you're an International Relations major and you're set to go overseas on a university-sponsored mission trip. This will help professionals see how in many respects your goals align in minimizing the challenges often associated with disability, even if there are other areas on which you disagree.

Faculty can also suggest the best logistics for achieving a goal in a research or service project. You could think of deficits in the services for disabilities based on your own background and propose new avenues to remedy them. For example, in medical school, I had wanted to do a broad survey on physician readiness on sensory issues in autism for physical examination. This was based on my own experience with piano for many years—the right touch is needed to produce the best sound. Although my sensory issues are fairly mild, I can appreciate how the sensory sensitivity of others might be barriers to effective health care. A physician cannot apply the same touch to each patient— just as a pianist cannot apply the same touch to every piano—and expect the same quality of outcome. Both doctors and pianists need to work on an individual basis to improve their art forms.

Professionals often know the system well and can provide realistic assessments of the challenges you might face as you implement ideas to start any disability advocacy or research project. Over time, your influence will likely enable them to take on a different view of disability. When I was involved with research and volunteering on campus, I was able to network with many professionals and was even able to even speak at annual autism conferences. I was given a chance to educate others by speaking about my own life, and I offered the advice that a positive, healthy, internalized autistic identity should ideally be in place before an autistic individual reaches the teenage years (autistic individuals are often negatively influenced by peer pressure). After my participation, the yearly events I spoke at began to include more autistic self-advocates in speaking positions. Now that's networking well done!

Some professionals continue to hold negative misconceptions about individuals with disabilities (e.g., people with disabilities are helpless and cannot self-advocate). If they make such statements in front of you or you have observed them making such statements in front of other people, please ask to make an appointment with the professional in private. When speaking with them about such issues, kindly address how such statements may lead to harmful misconceptions being propagated about people with disabilities. Do your research about the current state of a disability field to have some facts backing up your claims. Remind them about professional obligations to the autonomy and non-malfeasance that their clients are entitled to. To a person with a good compass for general morality, these measures may be enough to inspire change in his/her thinking patterns.

If a professional keeps up a pattern of overt condescension and humiliation of you or others like you, even after you've discussed the issue countless times, it might be wise to part on good terms. (If you have to work with this professional as part of a required class or internship you've committed for, I can say nothing more than to tolerate the experience and their quirks. Thereafter, you might offer your input to a designated organizational staff member that handles student affairs. They should be in the best position to listen to and respond to your feedback, and reporting of unprofessionalism is usually dealt with confidentially.) Most people really do mean well, and it is up to us to show them our potential for growth through working together.

In the end, you know yourself better than anyone else, including your own comfort in persevering and growing beyond your initial limitations. Professor Albus Dumbledore from the Harry Potter series summed it up best when he said, "It is our choices... that truly show what we are, far more than our abilities." Likewise, know yourself well and how far you are comfortable going in terms of forging ahead with your social interactions and life ambitions by either sticking with the skills you know well or moving beyond that initial comfort zone to see how far you'll go in any endeavor.

What Can the University do for You? Determining Your "ask"

By Elizabeth Boresow

This essay intends to explore what we (as advocates) can influence regarding University policies and actions through their administration.

Person-First Language

One area I would like to address is the move towards person-first language. Helping professions and many circles within the disability community are supporting the transition from identity based on disability (autistic kid, handicapped parking, stroke victim) to identity as a person before the disability (person with autism, accessible parking, stroke survivor). Everybody has personal preferences, but some organizations have taken stances for or against person-first language. The Deaf community prefers to be called deaf instead of hearing-impaired because impairment implies that something is wrong. One of my blind friends says it drives her crazy when people call her visually impaired because she is blind: she has no vision (her vision is not damaged, it just does not exist). The Arc supports person-first language when talking about people with Down syndrome and other intellectual and developmental disabilities. Many parents prefer person-first language when talking about their children. The autism community divides over this issue: autistic advocates tend to prefer "autistic" and view autism as part of an identity; parents tend to prefer hearing about their "children with autism." Please know that everybody has their own preferences and the best thing you can do is to respect your communication partner and their choice.

That being said, it is generally appropriate for institutions to use person-first language. One goal advocates may pursue is that a University's communications reflect person-first language. This includes their official statements, their policies, their signs, and their web sites. It is no longer considered appropriate to use the word "handicapped" – parking, seating, and restrooms are now designated "accessible."

Professional Development

Another area we can target is to add to or change the content of professional development in which faculty and staff participate. Adding training or practice on how to interact with people with disabilities can open up discussion. Here we can talk about person-first language. We can identify some of the main mistakes people make when interacting with PWD so that those mistakes are not made at the University. Teach staff about some of the barriers to effective communication and strategies to improve communication. Helping staff identify barriers to both communication and the general campus community can increase their understanding of the needs of the disability community and help them make their classrooms a more inclusive learning environment.

Centralization of Information

Having a central contact for disability-related information can be a big help and keep students, staff, faculty and visitors from being lost in a maze. One central contact can point people in the right direction for more specific information. This position exists at many schools and is often called an ADA coordinator. If this position or another does not exist at your school, it may be in the best interest of the school to create a position. This requires dialogue with many members of the administration, but it can be done. One would have to "pitch" the new position and explain why it is of benefit to the school. From there, someone in the administration should be able to point you in the right direction.

Another potential goal would be to compile resources about disability. This could include campus services, local services, and national services available to students and staff. Some campus resources could include the Disability Resources (possibly called Access Services or something else), a Disability Cultural Center (if it exists on your campus), a Multicultural Resource Center, the Health Center, tutoring services, and psychological services.

Big-Picture Planning

One of the easiest ways to make sure that disability is not forgotten in the University is to build recognition of disability into the University's diversity statement. Another way to ensure that the needs of people with disabilities are being met is to include people with disabilities on the various committees that exist within the University. There are certain types of committees where this will be more directly necessary (suppose you have a committee on technology, you will want to include someone on assistive technology) than others.

Build accountability into the University plans. Encourage student feedback about accessibility, perhaps through a survey at the end of the year. In the same way that students fill out course evaluations for professors at the end of the semester, consider having evaluation of advisors in the Disability Resources office or considering campus accessibility in general. Assign somebody the job of evaluating accessibility on campus, looking especially at construction on old buildings and construction of new buildings. This will help prevent problems if spaces are created within accepted standards the first time.

The last idea that I can convey about working with administration comes from an administrator at my University a few years ago. This administrator told me that his goal was to fulfill the *spirit of the law*, that is, the concept that the law attempts to articulate. The ADA intends to provide individuals access, so even if a situation is not clearly covered in the ADA requirements, this administrator's intent would be to follow the "spirit" of providing access and do what the University can to provide access. Conversely, some institutions follow the *letter of the law*, doing only what is exactly stated in the law and nothing more. By helping promote the former attitude of the *spirit of the law*, you can emphasize a common goal with the members of your University's administration. This common foundation can build a strong working relationship between advocates and administrators.

Interacting with Administrators

I can only offer up my experiences in hopes that you will find them useful in maintaining appropriate working relationships with the administrators who have the power to make lasting change at your University.

One area I work at is to wear appropriate attire. I have little skill in matching, but I have found that most of my peers are skilled in this department. Additionally, in order to communicate effectively I must be comfortable. The blend of these two needs that I have found works best is soft black slacks with a white t-shirt and a button-down blue or pink shirt over that. My wardrobe is small and the administrators have seen both of my dress-up shirts many times, but I feel that I have dressed appropriately and professionally. You must find what works for you. When in doubt, consider asking an adult in the work force for advice on clothing. Take their advice plus what you know about your own needs to try to find a compromise. Then, once you arrive at a meeting, you are free to focus on the primary task: working together towards realizing common goals.

To help ensure that all communications go smoothly, I am careful about the language and vocabulary I use. I stick to person-first language when referring to other individuals (with the exception of other individuals who have indicated they do _not_ prefer person-first language) and the disability community as a whole (except the Deaf and autistic advocacy groups). Many times, I take a second breath before I speak. Working with administrators who have a different set of priorities can be a frustrating experience, and I want to think through everything I say in order that my language is respectful. I refrain from placing blame on individuals and try to frame ideas in a positive manner. For example, I might talk about "upcoming sidewalk repairs" or "*the need for* upcoming sidewalk repairs" (instead of "all the broken sidewalks").

After a meeting, I like to send a follow up email. This ensures there is a paper record of the meeting. My letter will summarize what we talked about and thank the administrator(s) for taking the time to sit down and talk. In this way, we avoid miscommunications and summarize action statements of who is responsible for doing what.

Finally, I will close with a strategy statement on maintaining strong working relationships: look for common "ground" or mutual interests, goals that benefit all parties involved. Some of these goals include the University's desire to recruit a diverse mix of people to join the student body and work force (which benefits the advocate by having more representatives with disabilities) and making events accessible to the max number of people (and thereby allowing more people with disabilities to participate in such activities). Finding and explicitly communicating these benefits to your proposals helps entice the administration o work with you towards these goals.

Engaging on Accommodation and Service Provision Issues
By Elizabeth Boresow

One of the most powerful things you can do as a student group is give a strong voice from the disability community. This often means helping the University to realize that there are issues with the services being provided or that services are not being provided where they need to be.

For this to work, you must become familiar with your rights under the Americans with Disabilities Act. You can keep up to date with ADA information at www.ada.gov. You must also be familiar with your institution's policies and actual practices. Policies are the written rules of the institution. They tell you what is required of different parts of the institution. Your institution probably has a policy prohibiting sexual harassment, a policy prohibiting discrimination on the basis of disability, and policies regarding grade appeals, grievances, and research. Some policies affect all members of the university, and some are specific to students or faculty/staff or administration.

You must know about issues with accommodations in order to address them with administration. This is why you have a student group – the students can let you know when something is not working. For example, if the desk is not the correct height for someone that uses a wheelchair even after calling in and letting the administration know, you suddenly go from having one person who cares about an accommodation not being met to having a number of people that are concerned, and there is strength in numbers.

The last area of expertise you must develop is a knowledge of your institution. You should be able to find information online. Find out if you have an ADA Coordinator or one person that is designated as the "go-to" person for accessibility. At my University, that person is called the "Equal Opportunity Specialist / ADA & Title IX Coordinator," and he works in the Human Resources / Equal Opportunity Department. You can find information out like this by searching your school's website for "human resources" or "disability resources" or "ADA coordinator" or "accessibility." Asking someone from the Disability Resources office where to report concerns is the safest way to find the appropriate method for reporting accessibility concerns. What do you do if your University doesn't have one central contact for accessibility concerns? It is difficult to navigate a large institution to report different concerns with different departments, so I would recommend trying to get the University to designate somebody to fill that role. You can find out more about that process later.

It is important to document all issues and communications with University officials so there is a "paper trail," that is, a record of the issues and steps you have taken to report them and any communication you have received back. Email and letters are good forms of communication for this. Phone conversations can be harder to take record of – you must take good notes. You can ask permission to record meetings if that will be helpful to you. Your interactions must be both professional and polite. This may be difficult if you are frustrated, but refrain from name-calling or placing blame. Simply state the situation and what has or has not happened regarding the situation.

For example, say that one of your members is consistently visiting the library to find that the computer with JAWS screen-reader software is not working. That member has already reported to the library staff and the ADA Coordinator that the computer needs to be fixed. If no response has been received within three days, it is appropriate for you to send an email or make a phone call. I always prefer email simply because it gives me a better chance to get my thoughts together on paper and have another person make sure what I say makes sense – and there is a paper trail. Your email might look something like this:

> To Whom it May Concern:
>
> I would like to bring it to your attention that the accessible computer workstation at John Doe Library on the 4th floor by the snack machines is out of order. Although the log-on process works, opening a program such as Microsoft Word or Internet Explorer causes the computer to crash. I reported this to the library front desk last week and then sent an email to the ADA coordinator three days ago. I have not heard back from anyone on when this will be fixed.
>
> Please let me know when this will be fixed. It is hard to finish my research project when I cannot access the library resources. I appreciate your prompt attention to this matter.
>
> Sincerely,
> Elizabeth Boresow

If email is NOT your preferred response, be sure to provide the appropriate contact information. Communicate your appreciation for their attention to the situation. This shows your confidence in their ability to respond professionally, impelling them to respond (even if you don't *really* feel confident they will respond, you are appropriately assuming they will when you address them – this is good). Notice also the importance of providing enough information about what is going wrong. This may include sharing the exact location where the problem is, how or when you encounter the problem, and the dates surrounding the problem (when it started, when and how it was reported).

Another useful tip I have found is that telling more people makes more people accountable. When I send a letter like that, I send it to several people. I will choose a primary person and address them so that they know a response should primarily come from them. In this example, I would send it to the ADA Coordinator. I would use the carbon copy email function to include the Libraries ADA Specialist, my Disability Resources advisor, another officer from my student group, and the student group email (so that whoever runs the group years from now has a record of past problems and actions). In another situation where this carbon copy feature was effective, the primary email was sent to the woman in charge of Parking and Transit and copied to Disability Resources, the equivalent of an ADA Coordinator, the AbleHawks account, another AbleHawks officer, and two staff members that were likely to care about accessible parking because they also used wheelchairs. Having that many people involved in an email necessitated a response from the Parking and Transit woman.

Finally, be a known presence at your institution. This happens when you are prompt in reporting problems, responding to emails requesting more information, and act in a memorable manner. This could be either a good or bad reputation that you have, and it is important to present yourself so that you are known for your polite and professional manner of interaction. Nobody wants to help someone who complains without going through the proper channels. You will find that your interactions will be with some of the same people over time, especially the ADA coordinator. A good relationship with this person can expedite requests for repairs or changes to services provided.

In order to efficiently engage with administration on issues of accommodation and service provision, it is important to clearly articulate your concerns in a professional and timely fashion. These communications with the right people help the University to formally recognize problems and make them accountable for fixing the problems.

Creating a Disability Cultural Center

By Cara Liebowitz

As a disabled student attempting to create a Disability Cultural Center on her campus, I have found the process to be long, confusing, and full of Catch-22s. Before you begin the process of creating a Disability Cultural Center on your campus, you must ask yourself one question: *Why a Disability Cultural Center?*

College campuses around the country have ample resources and support for minorities on campus. My university alone has a Women's Center, a GLBTQ Center, and a whole building dedicated to the Multicultural Center. However, Disability Cultural Centers are usually glaringly absent from this litany of campus cultural hubs. Why?

The answer lies in the medical model of disability. Unlike race, gender, or sexual orientation, disability is not often seen as a unique minority group, with the ability to organize politically and socially. Disability is seen as an unfortunate event that *happens* to you, not a unique identity that *belongs* to you. As such, it is an internal matter that, in the eyes of the majority, must be dealt with privately, only trotted out to gain sympathy and pity. For these very reasons, disability can be profoundly isolating and extremely lonely. Ari Ne'eman, president of the Autistic Self-Advocacy Network, describes his experiences in this way:

> "One of the things I always appreciated about my first few weeks in college was the existence of the local Hillel — the Jewish student center active on my campus, and many hundreds of other campuses across the country. I was an out-of-state student going to a university where most of my classmates had grown up within no more than an hour's drive of the campus. Having an immediate sense of community as a Jew was incredibly meaningful for me — and yet, I always felt a profound sense of regret that I didn't have the same opportunities as an Autistic as I did as a Jew. Walking into the university disability services office was a far cry from the warmth of Shabbat dinner or outreach by campus Jewish organizations."

Many would argue that the disabled student population is already represented on most campuses, by the Disability Services Office. However, the DSO serves a very different purpose than a Disability Cultural Center. The DSO is required by law to provide academic accommodations to students with documented disabilities. The DSO is bound by confidentiality and cannot release the names of any students who receive their services. As a result, disabled students are often like planets in their own lonely orbits, utilizing the DSO, but never connecting with other disabled students on campus. One of the many purposes of a Disability Cultural Center is to connect students with disabilities to others who identify as such and to provide a safe space where disabled students, regardless of whether or not they receive services through the DSO, or whether they feel comfortable disclosing their disabilities to professors and nondisabled peers, can unite and share their experiences.

The need for a "safe space" – for any minority group – is extremely important. A Disability Cultural Center provides a place where students and staff with disabilities can convene to discuss the good, the bad, and the ugly aspects of disability. A Disability Cultural Center should strive to be welcoming of all identities, including, but not limited to, gender, race, and sexual orientation. After all, ableism interacts with every other –ism there is. Mia Mingus, disabled blogger and activist elaborates:

"Ableism cuts across all of our movements because ableism dictates how bodies should function against a mythical norm—an able-bodied standard of white supremacy, heterosexism, sexism, economic exploitation, moral/religious beliefs, age and ability. Ableism set the stage for queer and trans people to be institutionalized as mentally disabled; for communities of color to be understood as less capable, smart and intelligent, therefore "naturally" fit for slave labor; for women's bodies to be used to produce children, when, where and how men needed them; for people with disabilities to be seen as "disposable" in a capitalist and exploitative culture because we are not seen as "productive;" for immigrants to be thought of as a "disease" that we must "cure" because it is "weakening" our country; for violence, cycles of poverty, lack of resources and war to be used as systematic tools to construct disability in communities and entire countries."

There are people with disabilities in every minority group, from every background and class. The disability experience isn't limited to one stratum of people – it is universal.

So why should your administration approve of a Disability Cultural Center on campus? Two words: *recruit* and *retain*. Disability Cultural Center will *recruit* and *retain* students with disabilities. A crucial factor in picking a college, for a student with a disability, is how sensitive the school is to disability. Seemingly small things, like working automatic doors, or a friendly and supportive Disability Services staff, can make all the difference. A Disability Cultural Center on campus will be a beacon, a lighthouse for potential students, saying "We know about disability here. We understand. Come in and share your story." At the same time, it will offer a place where students who are already part of the campus can go to feel accepted and supported. Too often disability is equated with something bad or wrong, and being in an environment that sends that message, either implicitly or explicitly, can wreak havoc on a person's self esteem. A Disability Cultural Center can go a long way towards welcoming disabled students to your campus.

In addition, a Disability Cultural Center should be a resource, a place where students and staff with and without disabilities can go to learn about disabilities and various theories and ideas in the field of disability studies. A Disability Cultural Center – versus an awareness group on campus – is an actual, physical place that can feature a wealth of resources, all in one convenient place.

In conclusion, a Disability Cultural Center on a campus can benefit the entire campus community and make students and staff with disabilities feel more comfortable on campus.

Campaigns and Advocacy

A General Essay on Advocacy Goals and Priorities

By Leah Jane Grantham

I feel very blessed as a self-advocate. For me, being a self-advocate involves being part of something that's bigger than myself and my life, that allows me to participate in the shaping of not only my present situation, but the creation of a more positive future for those who will come after me. I remember seeing a poster once, which read, "Every barrier that autistic adults break down today is one that autistic children will not face tomorrow," which nicely sums up why I feel self-advocacy is so important and why I'm proud to be involved in it.

For me, being a self-advocate involves merging the personal with the political- I advocate for myself, but with the awareness that my self-advocacy could help set precedent, legally or socially, for others to get their rights a little easier. I also believe in lending my experiences and my advocacy to the personal struggles of others, because their burdens today will be the stones in a smooth road tomorrow. That's why, when asked, I will usually put my effort into advocating for others, such as being a silent witness, offering advice, and (like right now) writing about my history, perspectives, and ideas towards bringing about a less ableist, more inclusive world. Collaboration with other self-advocates and helping them advance their own goals is profoundly tied into my notion of self-advocacy, because I know that I benefit from their victories as much as they do from mine.

Everybody has a different story for how they came into self-advocacy; some did it after one final barrier proved to be the so-called "last straw," and some came into it after getting diagnosed/ realizing their disability, or after becoming political in other areas and discovering self-advocacy in the disability community. The way that you come into the world of self-advocacy is more than likely to influence how you formulate your goals, and how you intend to reach them. I'll share my own story to give an idea of how that scenario may play out.

My own journey into self-advocacy began when I became political at university. I had cynically and steadfastly avoided all political activity in high school, for several reasons. Most notably, I mistrusted the motivations of my classmates, believing that they didn't actually have a heartfelt commitment to the causes they supported, but were simply looking for a way to pad their college applications with impressive volunteer work. That struck me as being especially dishonest and phony, a means of projecting false modesty and false virtue in order to further one's own life.

I also felt, for the most part, helpless politically, believing that there was no way I could make a difference. I changed my tune, however, when I arrived at university. Now I didn't need to worry about impressing admissions boards, so I felt like I could be true to the type of activism I would be interested in doing, especially since it would be close to my heart and not done to impress someone else. Secondly, going to university in a highly political town with a long history of students doing what they could to turn the political tides and gain huge victories for their rights and the rights of others gave me hope for my own power.

I joined in many campaigns, and most memorably, I got deeply involved in Lesbian Gay Bisexual Transgendered Queer/Questioning (LGBTQ) and reproductive justice advocacy, along with anti-violence work.

I also joined the local autism club, but I didn't consider that to be political, because it was more of a social club. We received a visit from a representative from ADAPT, who was looking to recruit an autistic person for a special project that involved disabled people participating in the creation of research questions for a survey on violence against women with disabilities. I volunteered, because I thought my own experiences as a disabled person who lived through violent, traumatizing encounters might be helpful.

Volunteering with ADAPT was like an advocacy gateway drug. Once I got started with them, I couldn't stop. It was through ADAPT that I learned about how credos like "Nothing about us without us", intersectionality (how different biological, social, and cultural categories such as gender, race, class, ability, sexual orientation, and other types of identity contribute to social inequality), and the power of letting people have autonomy over their own lives are applied to a disability context. I'd never considered it through a disability lens before, and the lessons of ADAPT, and learning the history of self-advocacy, rocked my world. I now strive to use cooperation, collaboration, and activism to bring about my goals and see the world change the way I'd like to.

Think back to your own history, your own experiences, and your life. Chances are, they shape the way that you look at your place as an advocate and what your goals and priorities in disability advocacy are. No goal or priority has top value over all others on the universal scale, or on the individual scale. What truly matters is what makes you come to life and gets you passionate and ready to see things change. These are important things to keep in mind when getting involved with advocacy on a campus or in any life situation.

Working with Other Student Groups
by Allegra Stout

Whether you are implementing a protest, meeting with administrators, hosting a film screening, or planning any other activity to meet your group's goals, working with other student groups can be crucial. In this section, I discuss some of the reasons to work with other groups and ways to build mutually beneficial relationships.

Why seek other groups' support?

There is power in numbers. When trying to create change or get what your group needs, members of the administration and others are more likely to pay attention to the demands of a larger number of students. Two or more student groups working together often have even more power than their members would if they were all in one group, as the alliance shows that you are serious about meeting this goal and that it has support beyond one particular interest group.

You can reach a larger and more diverse audience. When one group advertises a campaign or an event, often only people who already feel comfortable with or interested in that group will participate. For example, if a disability student group hosts a social gathering like a board game night (perhaps with the intention of creating sensory-friendly social spaces), non-disabled students may assume that it is not really for them, even if the advertising says that everyone is welcome. At the same time, disabled students may fear that attending would amount to disclosing their disabilities. If the event is instead planned and advertised by the disability student group and another group, people may realize that it really is meant for everyone.

Your own group can become more inclusive of students' overlapping identities. No disabled student is exclusively disabled. We all have many other identities, such as race, class, gender identity, and sexual orientation, as well as other interests, like sports and academic subjects. Working with student groups dedicated to these other identities and interests can help make your group a safe space for all students with disabilities. For this to happen, your group must be willing to learn from other groups and change how you do things, not just put their names as co-sponsors on fliers.

You can help other groups become more accessible. In the process of working together, you may have opportunities to educate other groups about the importance of accessibility and different ways of achieving it. For example, during a shared meeting, members of the other group may comment on your group's clear communication and agenda. By explaining that these tools help members with diverse learning and social styles stay on the same page, you may inspire the other group to adopt similar techniques, or to have discussions about other access needs.

How can you build relationships with other groups?

Student groups support one another in countless ways, varying in formality, duration, intensity, and purpose. A very brief and low-intensity form of support might consist of the members of one group signing petitions for another. A much longer-lasting, more involved form of support could be a coalition of several groups who send delegates to one another's meetings, carry out projects together, and have regular joint meetings. Each relationship serves different needs. It often helps to discuss your group's reasons for reaching out to another group and plan how you would like the interaction to go, but also try to stay open to new directions that may emerge and to the needs of the other group. Alliances should be mutually beneficial, so if you seek the support of another group, be ready to be there for that group in turn.

One of the first steps is to decide which group(s) to contact. In some cases this happens naturally, as when a member of your group starts talking informally with members of another group about all that could be accomplished by joining forces. Otherwise, you might hold a brainstorming session in which members of your group share ideas about other campus groups. Some of your members are likely also active in other groups, and these might be a natural place to start. Perhaps you have heard of interesting events or political campaigns planned by a certain group. Additionally, most schools have lists of clubs and associations through which you can browse.

The type of support you are looking for impacts what type of group is best to contact. For example, a chess club might be delighted to co-host a board games night, but might not be interested in planning a campaign for accessible buildings. A wide variety of groups might be willing to help in ways that don't take much time, such as by signing a petition. If you reach out to a group for this kind of one-time support, however, emphasize that you are not looking for charity or pity, but rather for political support of your minority group. If you are seeking more substantial support, look for groups whose missions overlap more with yours, such as those working for human rights or advancing the cause of another identity group on campus.

Other groups that focus on disability issues may seem like obvious allies, but be careful to learn more about their goals and perspectives before trying to join forces. For example, volunteer groups may operate on a charity model of disability and see people with disabilities mainly as individuals who need help, rather than as a minority group struggling for equality. This doesn't mean you can't work with such a group; in fact, doing so may present a unique opportunity to introduce its members to new ways of thinking about disability. You might want to be careful, though, to limit your collaboration to specific projects on which your ideas really do mesh.

When first making contact, it helps to have a personal connection. This might be an individual who is part of both groups, a member of your group who has friends in the other group, or a professor who advises both. This contact can introduce you to leaders of the other group. If you can't find any personal connections, see if the group has a website with contact information or if your school has a list of contact people for student groups.

Regardless of how you find your contact, and whether you meet in person or talk by phone or email, start by explaining who you are, what your group does, how this is connected to their group, and what you would like from them. It also helps to show that you have some understanding of their group, such as by mentioning something they have done that you admire. It is also a good idea to ask if there is anything your group can do to help theirs.

If the response is favorable and some sort of relationship is established, you might want to help both groups learn more about the other. Consider asking if you can send a representative to one of their meetings to talk about your group, and ask if they would like to do the same. In some cases, it may make sense to have a representative of each group regularly attend the other's meetings and report back.

If you are looking for a long-term alliance, find ways to keep the lines of communication open beyond individual projects. You might want to designate someone to regularly check in with the other group. Information about relationships with other groups and the history of your work together can easily be lost when you and other leaders leave, so keep a regularly updated record of your group's allies.

Especially when working with other identity-based groups, take steps to educate yourself and your members to become better allies. If your disability group is mostly made up of white people and you are trying to work with a group of people of color, for example, learn about being an anti-racist ally through online resources, books, and any workshops that may be available. It may be useful to look for ways in which racism functions similarly to ableism, but remember that these issues are distinct in many ways. Once a relationship is established, it may be appropriate to ask your allied group if they can suggest ways to become better allies, but don't expect them to take responsibility for your education.

Conversely, if the members of a group with which you are trying to work don't seem to understand disability issues, try to educate them respectfully. The best way of doing this depends on the situation. Sometimes private conversations work well, and other times group presentations or workshops are better. You may want to suggest books, blogs, and other resources.

Working with other student groups is a vital part of student organizing, with unique rewards. I hope that the ideas in this section will help you build and strengthen relationships with other groups on your campus.

Pushing for Change in a Campus Policy
By Elizabeth Boresow

If you want to change a campus policy, you need a reason why it should change. To do this, you must show the University why the policy is ineffective. This could entail putting together and submitting a report summarizing the situation. Clearly document the problem and why it is a problem, even though this is redundant. For example, if your University's English course substitution policy requires you fail an English class (not essential to your major) three times before you are considered for a course substitution (even when you have a documented language-related learning disability), you should spell out the policy and the harm it does students. Such a policy ineffectively addresses the needs of students because of the excessive financial burden required to take a course three times as well as the self-esteem blow it is for a student to take a course and fail a course three times (to be told they must fail this many times in order to be considered for a course substitution).

Next, you must gather support from your campus. Surveys or petitions around campus are great ways to find out if you can get such support from your campus community. You can also look at institutions of similar size and status to see how their policies are different. You may find that there is another institution's policy that seems to work well, and you could provide this information as a suggested model to your institution. Establish contact with a University official such as your ADA Coordinator and ask them about the process for instigating a policy change. Likely, it will have to go through Student Senate. It is good to have a Student Senate representative from your group or one that can represent your cause. If you are having trouble understanding the process for a policy change, search your University's web site to find out who the Student Senate President is. This person will usually be reliable checking their email, so you can email them and ask for them to explain the process or refer you to someone else who can do this.

Look at the policy you are trying to change. Isolate the problem sections and draft what the changes need to look like. Then you can send it through the appropriate channels for review. Interactions with University officials and Student Senate members can help you understand what changes are feasible. Your input will help them because they may not have any idea about the inefficiencies of the policy. Be open and receptive to feedback about your draft and continue to work with others to edit the policy until all parties are satisfied. The review process can take time, so be patient and polite because other people are taking the time to listen to your concerns and work with you to improve the policy. Remember that you are trying to make a change that will benefit students for years to come and although things may not end up exactly as you imagined, the goal is always to make the campus policies more fair and accessible for all students.

Promoting New Policies around Disability

By Elizabeth Boresow

Specific structural changes or specific policy changes are a valuable part of advocacy. Despite that, problems may continue to exist until changes in the thought process are instigated. For example, an old building may not have any accessible restrooms. Changes to this restroom will be helpful but if the University policies do not require hiring contractors that perform work that is up to ADA standards, the problem will continue to exist. A policy may need to be added that specifies that all University subcontractors perform work that will be in compliance with the ADA, a new policy that requires the ADA coordinator to check in with subcontractors or on actual construction plans to ensure compliance. In another example, there is a problem when maintenance workers shovel snow piles in front of curb cuts. Removing the snow in front of a curb cut is a temporary fix to a problem that will likely recur without adding a policy. In this instance, the policy addition might revolve around the education of maintenance workers on why it is important that curb cuts remain clear during snow removal.

To convey the importance of an additional policy, you need to compile information about why the policy is needed. This could be pictures of inaccessible places or snow piles that block curb cuts. This could be reports from students of instances in which they were unable to enter a building because of snow piles, times they got stuck in a bathroom, or times when they were denied access to a campus bus. If it is possible to garner student support and/or faculty support for additional policies, this is a valuable additional resource. Surveys distributed on campus or petitions circulated are ways to gather support from your campus community.

Brainstorm as a group what new policies would be helpful to your members and community. Consider the feasibility of your ideas in terms of resources (manpower and money). Make a timeline for yourself that includes time for data collection, putting together the report, and different goals for having the policy submitted, reviewed, revised, and published. You may need to consult your University's Policy Library (it may be called Rules and Regulations) for how to get new policies approved. These policies should be listed online – search "policy" on your University's web site. Meeting with a University representative can often help you understand their perspective in terms of feasibility. It also helps to make them aware of the problems that inspire your thoughts of a new policy. They may be able to provide valuable insight on how to make your ideas a reality. Professionally interacting with them (and tracking your interactions via notes or email) gives you more credibility as a group with which they can consistently and reliably work on the issue at hand.

To promote policies around disability works the same way, except you have more to work with. You have the Americans with Disabilities Act that you can use to cite reasons why a policy is necessary. You also have a bunch of people across campus that you know will be interested in furthering policies around disability. The Disability Resources office, any disability-related student groups, groups of people majoring in helping fields (special education, music therapy, social welfare), and other diversity-related groups who represent minorities may be willing to lend support for your cause.

While I don't believe that it is your job as a student group to come up with "the answer" of how a policy will work, having organized goals can go a long ways towards making your wishes a reality. Make a plan, collaborate with University representatives and your campus community, compile the information into a professional looking report and stick to your plan to promote new policies. While the process is long, remember that the work you do will benefit generations to come.

Reversing a University Decision
By Elizabeth Boresow

When you feel like the decision of a University is unfair, you often have the right to appeal that decision. There are grade appeals and appeals of dismissal of complaints and grievances. The most important thing to remember is that there is a specific procedure called the appeals process. This process is strictly enforced to happen in a timely manner. Therefore, once you consider appealing a decision, it is imperative that you locate the appeals process relevant to your situation.

Different schools have different appeals processes, and you must navigate your University's Policy Library or Rules and Regulations (found on your University's web site). I will admit that doing this, even knowing what you are looking for and where to find it, is quite confusing. See if your institution has an Omsbud (search "omsbud" on the University web site). An Omsbud is a neutral, confidential, informal resource for anybody at a University to come to with concerns. This Omsbud is familiar with University policies and can help you assess your options. They can help you locate the specific appeals process you are looking for. Know that appeals processes may vary for graduate students, undergraduate students, faculty and staff, and unclassified staff as well as for what type of decision you are appealing.

Once you locate that policy, determine how long you have to write your appeals letter and who the appeal goes to. These will be explicitly stated in the policy. Draft a professional letter that covers all terms the policy says needs to be in the letter (the situation, the decision the University came to, on what grounds you are appealing, and why you believe the University's decision was erroneous).

Write formally (no contractions) and remember to include your contact information and the date. You will want to include a copy of the letter from the University that contains the decision you are trying to reverse. Before you send your letter, be sure to spell-check it and have someone else check it to make sure it is professional and appropriate. Refrain from making a personal story – speak of policy violations objectively. Additionally, be sure to speak respectfully of the University and convey your appreciation for its attention to the matter at hand. You may be asked to send a copy of the letter to the University body or representative that made the initial decision you are appealing. Sign your letters (either in pen or electronically) and keep a copy for your reference. You will then hear back from the person you addressed the letter with further instruction on how the process works. This person should give you a decision and will let you know if any further action from you is possible or necessary. Remember that no matter the decision, you must remain respectful of all parties involved.

For example, if you took a general psychology course at KU and wanted to appeal the grade, you would have to search the Policy Library online for the Undergraduate CLAS (College of Liberal Arts and Sciences) Policy for Grade Appeals. You would follow the steps and list why the grade received is erroneous. Maybe the instructor did not assign grades the way his syllabus stated he would. You would address the letter to the Chairperson of the Psychology Department. From there, you would wait for a response.

Addressing a Specific Discriminatory Faculty or Staff Member

By Elizabeth Boresow

Unfortunately, there are times when a specific faculty or staff member at your institution may discriminate against you because you have a disability. The ADA prohibits discrimination on the basis of disability. Your University probably has policies that explicitly prohibit such discrimination. If you feel like you have a problem with a faculty or staff member, the first thing you should do is let them know. There are informal and formal ways of addressing discrimination; everyone prefers informal. Policies often state that your first step before filing any paperwork is to speak with your professor (or whomever) to discuss the concerns. This can be a tricky conversation, especially if you have already been made uncomfortable by such a professor. This is when I return to the old standby of a written interaction. Write or type a note that explains why you feel like you have been discriminated against and how you would like that to stop. Keep a copy for your records.

January 6, 2012

Dear Professor Jones,

You have made several comments in our ABC 101 class about how lazy some students are when they leave after the fire drill causes a temporary stop to class. I feel bad when I hear those comments because I have shared with you that a fire alarm really hurts my ears and my head. The accommodations form you signed at the beginning of the semester says that if there is a fire drill, I will be excused from the rest of classes that day. I am not lazy and I feel bad when my classmates see me leave and hear the next class period about how people who don't come back to class after the drill ends are lazy. Neither of us like the fact that the construction crew keeps setting off alarms in the building. It would mean a lot to me if you could refrain from making those comments in class.

Thanks,
Elizabeth Boresow

That was just one made up example. Those comments may or may not have been directed at you, but they were inappropriate considering your accommodation. This letter could be emailed or handed off in person. In fact, if you are a more confident speaker than myself, you could just go have a conversation with your professor rather thancommunicating the information in the letter to her.

In response, your professor could apologize, explaining that she didn't realize her comments upset you. In this case, graciously accept her apology and go about the rest of the semester. You may want to ask her if she will clear up the fact that you are not lazy and that you are receiving an accommodation because of your hearing. Such a request could go into your letter and the professor may be willing to do this. The professor may not respond (or seem to be ignoring you) – this could be okay, if you didn't explicitly ask for a response. If the professor makes such comments again, remind her about the letter you sent. The last response your professor might have is to ridicule your letter or deliberately continue to make such comments. This occasion would be rare, although it can happen.

If the issue hasn't been resolved in this informal yet professional way, your next bet is the University Omsbud. The Omsbud will be able to help you explore your options before you take any official action. The Omsbud will also be able to direct you towards the complaint or grievance process. If your institution does not have an Omsbud, you can contact the Human Resources Department for information on how to handle complaints of discrimination. There will likely be time constraints for when you must start the complaint process, so check what the policy says about time requirements. Another way to find this policy is to check your University's anti-discrimination policy, which can be found online through your school's Policy Library or Rules and Regulations. It should state what your rights are if you believe you have been discriminated against. It also becomes important to document instances in which you are discriminated against. If you can start a paper trail, something as simple as a log of times when your professor makes inappropriate comments and your responses to him, this will give you a record of consistent documentation showing a pattern of inappropriate conduct.

If you decide to continue on with a formal complaint, you will need to write a letter to notify the appropriate authority that you wish to file a complaint. The relevant policy should specify what the letter includes, such as the name of the discriminatory University representative and what discriminatory actions or statements have occurred with their frequency and their consequences for you. For example, at my University you file complaints of discrimination through the Human Resources/Equal Opportunity (HR/EO) office. You would provide your logs and copies of letters or written interactions you have had with the individual in question with HR/EO, and it will investigate the complaint and either dismiss it or take action based on it.

It is important that you do not let anger show in such complaints. As much as you have the right to be angry about being discriminated against, you need to *objectively* state that the anti-discrimination policy has been violated and *objectively* detail how your rights have been violated and that such violation has caused you distinct injury (it does not have to be physical injury).

Hopefully, you will not feel so seriously discriminated against that you need to take action against a specific member of your institution. Most matters are simply issues of ignorance that can be fixed with clear and appropriate communication between two adults such as yourself and the University member. In the case that you do feel it necessary to take further action, remember to make a paper trail by way of a log and use your campus resources such as the Omsbud, Student Legal Services, and the University web site to help you evaluate your options and file the written complaint in a timely manner. I hope that you will be able to come to an agreeable resolution that is beneficial and fair for all individuals involved.

What is Disability Studies?

Advocating for Disability Studies as Part of Systems Change
By Allegra Stout

In my work to create a more accessible and inclusive campus, I have found that what I like to call "academic advocacy," or advocating for the incorporation of Disability Studies into the curriculum, is a very useful tool. In this section, I briefly explain what Disability Studies is, why it is important for systems change, what forms academic advocacy can take, and where to find a few useful resources.

What is Disability Studies?

Chances are that even if your school has no Disability Studies classes, the subject of disability comes up frequently in a variety of disciplines. Abnormal Psychology classes focus on the symptoms and treatment of psychiatric disabilities, biology classes include information about chromosomal differences and genetic mutations, and English classes discuss disabled characters. These approaches may include useful information, but they also frequently include harmful assumptions, as when teachers of literature uncritically reinforce associations between walking with a limp and being a villain.

Disability Studies, then, does not just mean studying disabilities or disabled people. Instead, it requires taking a particular perspective on disability. As Syracuse University's Center on Human Policy, Law, and Disability Studies explains,

> Disability Studies refers generally to the examination of disability as a social, cultural, and political phenomenon. In contrast to clinical, medical, or therapeutic perspectives on disability, Disability Studies focuses on how disability is defined and represented in society. It rejects the perception of disability as a functional impairment that limits a person's activities. From this perspective, disability is not a characteristic that exists in the person or a problem of the person that must be "fixed" or "cured." Instead, disability is a construct that finds its meaning within a social and cultural context. (http://disabilitystudies.syr.edu/what/whatis.aspx)

One crucial aspect of Disability Studies is the idea that there are different *models of disability*, or ways of understanding what disability is, and that each comes with its own sets of questions to ask and types of solutions. As mentioned above, academic models of disability include clinical, medical, and therapeutic perspectives. Medical models, for example, are prevalent in disciplines like biology and (obviously) medicine. People in these fields tend to see disability as something wrong with an individual person's body or mind, and to assume that the appropriate response is to try to fix or cure it. Many, though by no means all, Disability Studies scholars and disability rights activists use the *social model of disability*, which understands disability as arising not from individual flaws, but rather from a society that sets up barriers to access for people whose bodies and minds differ from the norm. According to this approach, the appropriate response to problems associated with disabilities is to change society and remove barriers.

Why is Disability Studies important for systems change?

When I tell people about my work to increase representation of Disability Studies in my school's curriculum, it's not always immediately obvious how that fits into the work of my disability rights group. After all, not all disabled people are interested in Disability Studies, and discussing theories in a classroom won't get more ramps built. To me, though, the theories and ideas taught in Disability Studies are a vital part of disability rights activism for several reasons.

First, Disability Studies provides a framework for understanding disabled people as an oppressed minority group and disability as an identity. This model is vital to the work of disability rights student groups and others working to improve access and fight ableism, for it prepares people to stop thinking in terms of pity and individual problems and start thinking in terms of rights and social justice. Disability Studies can provide a crucial alternative perspective on disability and introduce faculty, staff, and students to understandings of disability beyond those advanced by disability services offices or biology classes. This is very important not only for non-disabled community members, but also for disabled students ourselves, for many students arrive at college having never encountered the idea that they have something in common with other disabled people and that they can be proud to be part of a disability community, rather than be privately ashamed.

Second, Disability Studies increases understanding that many of the problems disabled people face are due to ableist environments and attitudes and thus can be ameliorated through systems change. This goes hand-in-hand with the previous point, for when people begin to understand disabled people as a minority group rather than a bunch of flawed individuals, they may begin to see that they should take steps to level the playing field and decrease discrimination against members of the group.

Third, Disability Studies includes a variety of more specific ideas that can transform people's thinking and help them understand disability or campus accessibility issues in a new light. For example, the idea of "universal design" means (in part) that buildings, products, classes, and everything else should be designed from the beginning to be as accessible as possible to people of all abilities. This concept can help you and other students explain to professors why they should incorporate accessibility features into their classes from the very first class, rather than wait for individual students to request accommodations.

All of these benefits (and the many more I won't try to list here!) can start with individual teachers and students doing Disability Studies work, but will then begin to have wider effects on the campus. For example, one student might take a Disability Studies class, then bring up the social model of disability later when a friend comments that all disabled people should be cured. Or a disability services provider might begin hearing from students about ideas from Disability Studies and begin to do some reading and change her own ideas. Like any academic discipline, Disability Studies can contribute to the overall campus culture and provide all members of a school community with valuable new perspectives.

What forms can academic advocacy take?

Advocating for Disability Studies doesn't have to mean demanding that a new major be created tomorrow (as great as that would be). There are several different options to consider, which require varying amounts of resources and bureaucracy. When pursuing any of these options, be sure to reach out to both disabled and non-disabled students and professors, for Disability Studies is fundamental to understanding our society for people of all ability statuses, and we need non-disabled allies who understand its principles.

Keep in mind that, since disability already comes up in a wide variety of fields, you may not need to create whole new classes in order to make a difference. Instead, you can encourage individual professors and departments to include Disability Studies perspectives within current course offerings. For example, an Abnormal Psychology professor might supplement his lesson on schizophrenia with a discussion of mad pride and other radical mental health movements and explain that the medical model is not the only way to understand mental illnesses. Or an African-American Studies professor might expand a course on eugenics to include some of the history of forced sterilization of disabled people, including many people of color.

When encouraging professors to incorporate Disability Studies into their syllabi, you can take several approaches. One is simply to meet with a professor whose class might overlap with Disability Studies, and explain the connections. It is usually more effective, though, for students who have actually taken the classes in question to talk to the professors, as they have better understandings of the professors' perspectives and the content of the classes. Another approach is to bring up Disability Studies perspectives in class whenever relevant, with the hope of encouraging the professor and other students to think seriously about them. For example, if you're taking a literature class that includes no discussion of the representations of characters' disabilities, you can thoughtfully bring this up. Be careful with this approach, though, as it can quickly become repetitive and begin to annoy the professor. You can also write papers or give class presentations about connections with ideas from Disability Studies and then meet afterward to talk to the professor about the possibility of incorporating the subject into future versions of the course.

Another form of academic advocacy can be bringing guest speakers or films about Disability Studies. This can be especially effective when working with an academic department. For example, my school's Feminist, Gender, and Sexuality Studies program has an annual symposium, and each year professors pick the topic based on student interest. Last year, partly because of the highly publicized efforts of my disability rights group, the program faculty decided to make the theme of the symposium "Feminist Disability Studies." A couple of other students and I helped select speakers, and a wide variety of faculty and students appreciated the opportunity to learn more about this topic. Several of the professors who attended took careful notes and expressed a desire to begin including Disability Studies ideas in their courses.

If your college has any opportunities for students to design and teach their own courses, this is another great way to increase interest in and understanding of Disability Studies. My school allows students to teach full-credit classes under the minimal supervision of a faculty adviser, so two years ago I worked with two friends to write a syllabus for and teach an Introduction to Disability Studies course, with eight students. This year, a younger student is teaching the course for a second time.

If your school doesn't yet have any Disability Studies courses, I suggest starting with the approaches above, in order to spark awareness of and interest in the field among faculty and students. As you progress, take care to develop good working relationships with any faculty or administrators who advise or help you along the way, and/or who show an interest in Disability Studies.

As time goes on, or if you are lucky enough to already have a few Disability Studies courses or professors who incorporate ideas from Disability Studies, you may want to start thinking on a bigger scale. Possibilities will vary widely depending on your school, but you may be able to provide input into faculty hiring processes, petition departments to add Disability Studies courses, or even advocate for the creation of an academic minor or department. When considering these options, or trying to figure out the processes involved, it always helps to seek advice from supportive faculty and administrators, who are likely to have more information about the inner workings of academic departments, and may be able to suggest next steps or people to contact. These approaches take much greater administrative and financial resources than working with individual professors or other students, but they also have the greatest potential to create lasting change for your campus.

Resources

Whatever your approach to advancing Disability Studies on your campus, here are just a few of the many rich online resources that may be helpful:

Society for Disability Studies (http://disstudies.org/) is a professional organization that hosts a website, a listserv, and an annual conference. Its "Guidelines for Disability Studies Programs" page is a very useful resource for understanding the parameters of Disability Studies and what it means to take a Disability Studies approach.

Disability Studies Quarterly (http://dsq-sds.org/) is a peer-reviewed academic journal. It can be useful for getting a sense of the types of questions and approaches that have been pursued in the field. It's highly interdisciplinary, so you may be able to find articles that can help convince professors in a wide variety of fields of the relevance of Disability Studies.

The website of *Disability Studies at Syracuse University* (http://disabilitystudies.syr.edu/what/disabilitystudiesatSU.aspx) includes a variety of helpful resources, including a description of Disability Studies, a list of academic programs in Disability Studies across the United States, and sample syllabi for Disability Studies courses.

Disability Studies: Information and Resources (http://thechp.syr.edu/Disability_Studies_2003_current.html) includes an extensive annotated bibliography of Disability Studies books, chapters, and articles.

Interactions between Theoretical Models and Practical Stakeholders: The Basis for an Integrative, Collaborative Approach to Disabilities

By Steven Kapp

The way society views and addresses disabilities and disabled people has changed dramatically in recent years and has approached a general paradigm. Led by the influence of the disability rights movement, disabilities now have become understood at least partly as a social construction and public matter, and few doctors will self-identify as proponents of a classical biomedical model. Meanwhile, disabled people increasingly call attention to and embrace the neurobiological origin of their conditions, often those that lack useful physical or biological markers or tests and thus invite controversy (Baker, 2011). Prior to learning about these issues informally as an undergraduate student in public policy beginning with a disabled (fellow Autistic self-advocate) mentor, and especially now as a PhD student in educational psychology researching related areas, I had little understanding of the biomedical model and no awareness of the advocacy-inspired social model of disability. Understanding the similarities and differences between the biomedical establishment and activists may help with practical advocacy efforts.

Biomedical model

A moral model dominated before the medical model (Weiner, 1993). Medical technology often included nothing more than basic physical examination, so listening to the patient's history had paramount importance and an intimate doctor-patient relationship formed the basis of healthcare. Lacking decisive expertise about the body, doctors relied heavily on lifestyles, beliefs, and the environmental context when making diagnoses and predicting the course of conditions (Bury, 2001). Yet the doctors often inaccurately viewed conditions as unnatural, with a personal or social cause, and society assigned even more moral responsibility and judgment to many disabilities or atypicalities. Intuitions, traditions, folklore, and misplaced religious beliefs often led laypeople to view unusual behavior as wicked or sinful, or otherwise exhibiting poor character. Accordingly, people with disabilities suffered exclusion, abuse, and other inhumane treatment in pervasive, basic but socially sanctioned ways (Weiner, 1993).

The modern Western biomedical model rose to relieve people of moral responsibility and to strengthen people's trust in the scientifically grounded knowledge and professional judgment of doctors and other providers (Brickman et al., 1982). The model arose in the mid- to late 1800s as modern hospitals and laboratories grew alongside – and sometimes in response to – immunizations against infectious diseases (Bury, 2001). For much of its history, it focused mainly on diseases and disabilities with clear physical causes. The dominance of psychoanalysis and behaviorism meant that psychologists often attributed psychiatrically diagnosed conditions – those without known causes and without clear effects on physical appearance – to environmental causes like poor parenting. The modern understanding of the brain began in the 1970s, and a broad, continuous, biopsychosocial model of so-called "mental disorders" became replaced with a symptom-based, categorical medical model (Wilson, 1993). The publication of the third edition of the main diagnostic classification system, the *Diagnostic and Statistical Manual (DSM)*, in 1980 cemented the shift (Mayes & Horwitz, 2005). It created many more categories, and the *DSM-IV* in 1994, the edition in use today, built on its predecessor.

As the name implies, the model tends to attribute biological causes to health conditions and disabilities, replacing a goal of restoring people to natural conditions with making them normal, based on statistical deviation from the average (Bury, 2001). This becomes a problem when natural differences may have inherent strengths or at least neutral function, and when normal functioning lacks anything inherently better or good. This can lead to a confirmation bias that pathologizes extreme differences between typical and disabled people, whether observed in the biology or behavior, without considering the possibly adaptive function they may serve. The medical nature of this deficit basis also potentially groups together all people with unusual functioning or health issues as "sick," "diseased," or "broken," without distinguishing between challenging but stable, non-injurious conditions that may ease over time, and degenerative, fatal, and otherwise obviously harmful problems. The biological essence of the model relates to the traditional view of people as a collection of organs (sometimes measured behaviorally as "symptoms") and its separation of the mind, body, and what some might call the spirit (Brickman et al., 1982). Yet they work together, as shown by the placebo effect, where people's health improves (or they perceive that it does) based on taking a "treatment" that lacks the direct ability to help. Moreover, the model's overemphasis of biology means that it ignores the contribution that the environment (such as culture and family) and personal characteristics beyond the condition (such as factors more closely related to self-determination, including motivation) may play in their effect on the person (Putnam,.2005; Shakespeare, 2008).

Despite potential protections the biomedical model offers from the moral model, it has the potential for its own form of oppression. Its view of people as submissive "patients" compliant with medical authority as the source of all knowledge deprives laypeople of the self-determination to make their own decisions based on comprehensive access to information. A "professional knows best" paternalism, however benevolent in its intentions, obscures medicine's reality as an art in addition to a science, with risks and uncertainties, and various possible combination of costs and benefits, associated with a wide array of choices (Groopman & Hartzband, 2011). People's circumstances, lifestyles, values, and preferences affect their health, and they must exert self-determination as active agents in control over their lives for optimal outcomes.

Indeed, a pure medical model does not make sense for disabilities, as it lacks nuance and disempowers people. Its success with vaccines helped to establish it, and current sociocultural resistance to childhood vaccinations for various scientifically unfounded reasons and with harmful – even deadly – consequences reveal the need for continued confidence in the medical model where it offers such decisive solutions. Yet, in an absolute form, the model can pose dangers for disabled people. The emphasis on causation, prevention, and cure does not improve the quality of life of disabled people now and contrasts with the opposition of some disabled people and our allies. The emphasis on treatment often lacks sensitivity to the complex problems with the medical model, such as normalization for its own sake rather than quality of life, and often means insufficient attention to what it might call "management" and care (social support, assistive technology, coping mechanisms, other help through services and accommodations, and so on). Moreover, the notion of disability as a personal tragedy fosters dependency on professionals, not finding fault in ineffective and even abusive interventions for people deemed helpless (Brickman et al., 1982). It also fosters dependency on greater society through pity and charity (Shapiro, 1993).

Social model of disability

Alternative understandings of disability grew primarily from the disability rights movement's resistance to the biomedical model. Emerging in the 1960s from the civil rights movement, the movement's disabled people and allies have emphasized the exclusions and barriers posed by society. Accordingly, factors such as discriminatory attitudes and physically or cognitively inaccessible environments contribute to, if not create, disability. The movement has promoted basic human rights to prevent and address discrimination against disabled people and enable reasonable accommodations, for people to participate fully in educational, employment, independent living, and other opportunities with appropriate support (Shapiro, 1993). Its motto, "Nothing About Us Without Us!" refers to the need to fully include disabled people in all matters that directly affect us, such as advocacy organizations, the media, the arts, and research (Charlton, 1998).

A social model of disability began that originally took an absolute position that the environment alone creates disability. It first became clearly articulated in the United Kingdom in 1975 by the Union of the Physically Impaired Against Segregation, a disability rights organization. The classic social model makes a simple distinction between *impairment* internal to the mind or body and *disability* created by an oppressive society. Such a pure model made more sense before the creation of basic civil rights laws when disabled people often lacked the legal right to an education, to work, and to live in the community rather than institutions. Those dehumanizing injustices pose unjust problems for people that seem more obvious today, although much room for progress remains. It also has a more straightforward application for some disabilities, such as certain mobility disabilities that, with assistive technology like wheelchairs and architectural adaptations like elevators, ramps, and curb cuts, may pose more readily accommodated limitations to the people's participation in society (Shakespeare, 2008).

More progressive, nuanced forms of the social model acknowledge that for many disabilities impairment itself has a major social component. Affected functions often lie on a continuum with typical functioning, or the unusual traits depend on the context for their manifestation or functioning as a strength, weakness, or just difference. Certain abilities fluctuate in relevance over time; reading abilities, for example, have now become viewed as critical to success, but in preliterate times dyslexia may not have disabled people (Armstrong, 2010). Some have tried to universalize or eliminate the clinical notion of disability by correctly pointing out the interdependencies, limitations, and environmental effects that bond all people.

While some conditions for some people also present great challenges regardless of the social context, studying and understanding this in practice provides its own obstacles. Natural or bodily and social influences can seem impossible to disentangle. As people develop, age, or learn to live with their disability, the condition itself may change over time for complex reasons. Disabled people may thus serve as the best source for describing the effect of the condition on their lives. The medical model challenges this viewpoint by suggesting that certain disabilities it regards as severe render people unable to reliably self-report. Social model thinkers counter that in the absence of absolutely definitive evidence, we must make the least dangerous assumption of presuming competence (Donnellan, 1984).

Tests generally measure what people can do, rather than what they supposedly cannot do; many issues unrelated to the test may interfere with people's measured performance, such as time, anxiety or mood, motivation, attention, language, culture, and behavioral differences. Reflecting the problems with IQ testing, the proposed revision of the diagnosis of intellectual disability acknowledges that a low test score alone does not determine disability and that the tests disadvantage cultural minorities. The rise of the self-advocacy movement has shifted the paradigm of understanding intellectual and other disabilities, promoting practices for people to exert self-determination or take control over their lives across the full spectrum of intellectual ability, and challenging practitioners to measure and support everyone to have what they perceive as a high quality of life for themselves (Petry & Maes, 2009). With the growth of augmentative and alternative communication technologies, more people can demonstrate their abilities and access reliable communication, regardless of speech or language.

Disability studies has risen as an interdisciplinary academic field to address such matters of the relationship between disabled people and society. It often has adopted the social model, but ultimately seeks to understand how disabled people make sense of their own lives. Such research has found that many disabled people view their condition as directly disabling (Beachamp-Pryor, 2011). Indeed, some early proponents of the social model suggest they considered it a starting point of inquiry rather than something to consider or implement in an unconditional form. By the late 1990s and early 2000s, many disability scholars called for skepticism or rejection of a pure social model, and several have offered alternatives that lie between it and the pure biomedical model (Darling & Heckert, 2010a; Shakespeare, 2008).

Interactive models of disability

Thanks in large part to the disability rights movement, the medical and social models have moved toward one another and interactionist models gain momentum in research and dominate in practice, likely reflecting that reality lies somewhere between the extremes. In the late 1970s, around the time the biomedical model became most formulated into the *DSM*, medical researchers and practitioners began to publish on a biopsychosocial model (Engel, 1977). In theory, the model means that biological (such as the basis of conditions), psychological (thoughts and emotions that do not necessarily originate from a condition), and social (such as stigma and the surrounding community) factors all contribute to functioning (and impairment, when present, that interferes with adaptive functioning or daily living).

In practice, the model means that the client and provider form a connection or relationship that involves the provider's incorporation of the client's subjective experience for more personalized care (Borrell-Carrió , Suchman, & Epstein, 2004). It has taken a few forms, and the general paradigm has contributed to many fields. Perhaps the most authoritative, detailed variant underlies the World Health Organization's *International Classification of Functioning, Disability, and Health (ICF)*. The *ICF* conceptualizes and measures disability as an interaction between the specific condition, other personal characteristics, and the environment. It complements the *International Classification of Diseases*, which like the *DSM* currently, lists symptom-based categories as diagnoses.

Now a biopsychosocial model in origin of and response to disability prevails in the medical and clinical fields (Lechman & March, 2011; Palmer & Handley, in press; Rutter, Moffit, & Caspi, 2006). Today professionals often would often disagree that they staunchly follow a pure form of the medical model (Baker, 2011). Many reasons account for this change. The disability and other civil rights movements, and perhaps often cultural phenomena like the digital revolution or globalization, have resulted in a more open, less hierarchical society where more people take ownership of their needs and resist playing the traditional "sick" or "patient" role. Certainly, the proliferation of the media and information on the Internet have produced more democratic self-empowerment. Unprecedented access to information, along with the rising cost of high-tech medicine, also leads more people to counter the establishment with alternative medicine or lifestyles (including vitamins, supplements, specialized diets, meditation, and deep breathing; Bury, 2001). Mainstream doctors have started to accept many alternative or holistic practices as complementary rather than in opposition to their work (Astin, Shapiro, Eisenberg, & Forys, 2003), and psychologists have a recent surge of interest in mindfulness for stress reduction and everyday living. Healthcare reform in the United States probably increases priorities around primary care, furthering a trend toward holistic medicine and giving less power to disease-minded specialists.

Disability scholars and activists also continue to address the main criticisms of the pure social model, such as that it lacks sensitivity to many disabled people's actual perspectives and to the specific nature of conditions. Among the alternative models proposed, the affirmative model, built on disability identity and culture, asserts impairment as an equally valid form of human diversity. While a pure social model brings the attention only to society, possibly suggesting nothing inherently valuable about the underlying condition, the affirmative model retains some social focus but also looks within conditions to celebrate or at least legitimize them (Swain & French, 2000).

Similarly, research has indicated some factors that affect the likelihood that people view their disability as a positive part of identity and oppose a cure (Putnam, 2005). This includes age of the condition's onset, with – not surprisingly – people who have grown up with a disability or acquired it early in life more likely to have a proud disability identity (Hahn & Belt, 2004; Darling & Heckert, 2010b) and reject treatment toward a cure (Hahn & Belt, 2004). They are more likely to report better health (Jamoom et al., 2008) and not view themselves as severely disabled (Darling & Heckert, 2010a). Although youth aware of their disability often do not identify with other disabled people (Darling & Heckert, 2010b), this may result from lack of access related to an inclusive environment; once they meet other disabled people like them or become aware of disability rights or pride groups, their views often move toward neurodiversity (Griffin & Pollack, 2009). Similarly, disability rights leaders often drew inspiration for their activism from meeting other leaders (McCarthy, 2003). The age of onset seems more important than age of awareness, because people who recognize and receive a diagnosis for their developmental disability (which, by definition, begins before age 21) as adults still may find it useful for their self-understanding and support (King et al., 2003). People who acquire disability in adulthood tend to begin from a place of tragedy but often learn to renegotiate their values and goals based on the new challenges in their life (Galvin, 2005). People who become disabled late in life usually perceive the onset of disability as less disruptive than those who acquire disability in earlier adulthood, but also tend to view it as a normal part of the aging process, with less likelihood of developing it into a proactive identity (Lawton, 2003).

Neurodiversity has the potential as both a philosophy (Armstrong, 2010) and movement (Baker, 2011) to offer a vision forward for an influential, integrative model of disability. It refers to disabilities as a natural, equally acceptable part of human diversity, with a focus on quality of life rather than causation and cure. *Objective quality of life* refers to adaptive functioning in contexts such a social relationships, education, employment, and daily living. *Subjective quality of life* or *subjective well-being* means the happiness and satisfaction that people feel about their lives. Neurodiversity also builds on the fact that conditions sometimes offer selective advantages as well as offer some traits that do not necessarily present inherent problems. Altogether it allows for therapies or other interventions (preferably called *treatments* in the medical model) to mitigate aspects of the condition that may threaten quality of life, in addition to services and accommodations that work around challenges and build on strengths, while expecting a person-centered approach that allows or empowers as much self-determination as possible.

While the movement currently has no clear boundaries of what conditions it includes, it may have wide applicability. Although often applied to the autism spectrum, a broader array of disabled people and professionals increasingly has extended it to other disabilities that – like autism – affect cognition, emotions, sensation, and movement. The brain links the mind to the body, suggesting that neurodiveristy may refer not only to developmental, learning, and mental health disabilities, but also sensory and mobility disabilities. Psychiatry, which addresses disabilities that lack a known cause, diagnoses based on behavior and labels conditions "mental," historically pathologizing people as *deficient* (lacking basic competence) or *deviant* (violating social norms, possibly immoral or dangerous). Yet understanding the interconnection between the mind and the body may suggest people act as dynamic systems, who need rhythm and balance to self-regulate (Donnellan, Hill, & Leary, 2010). People thus need contextualized integration, flexibility, regulation, and coordination when processing information, and unusual neurological wiring does not necessarily mean absence or dysfunction. Behaviors may serve different functions for different people and whether and how they convey the intended message or reflect self-control varies remarkably (Donnellan et al., 2010).

Psychiatric classifications may soon undergo a revolution that conceptually may bring the field closer to neurodiversity, but presents risks in addition to opportunities. Technically the medical model already recognizes disability as a natural – yet, it also claims, abnormal and unacceptable – part of the human experience. The proposed *DSM-5* would also place disabilities on a spectrum of natural variation.

Psychiatrists have recognized that their categorical medical model lacks scientific evidence (Anckarsäter, 2010; Hyman, 2010). A categorical classification system assumes that the people assigned a diagnosis have a qualitative difference from the rest of humanity – that they have a fundamentally different experience from supposedly "normal" people, neatly fit their label, and clearly do not meet criteria for apparently similar conditions (Hyman, 2010). Yet most, if not virtually all, conditions in the system – perhaps in general – have quantitative differences, where the disability results from a constellation or cluster of common traits in certain degrees and combinations. Disabilities often lie on a universal spectrum or continuum, possessing fluid boundaries with other disabilities and the general population. This means that usually more people occupy a position closer to either side of a condition's "mild" edges where it becomes "subclinical" than to its extreme manifestations, that people with the same disability share much within-group diversity (medically referred to as heterogeneity), and that most people with a disability listed in the *DSM* meet criteria for multiple such disabilities (Anckarsäter, 2010; Hyman, 2010). Similarly, a disease model often assumes disabilities have a specific cause, like a virus or simple genetics, yet the biological bases have proven more complicated than scientists expected. The complex overlap between people labeled "pathological" and "healthy" exists not only in behavior (medically known as *phenotype*), but also neuropsychological mechanisms (*endophenotype*), and genes (*genotype*). Consequently, scientists have hardly discovered any definitive causes and still cannot use biological tests to prevent or diagnose psychiatrically registered disabilities (Hyman, 2010).

The *DSM-5* hopes to address these flaws by replacing categorical diagnoses with dimensional ones: introducing a severity scale, allowing for more co-occurring diagnoses (medically referred to as *comorbidities*, indicating the medical model's description of disability as taking away liveliness), and reconceptualizing impairment. A severity scale misses the separability of traits or "symptoms" – a person may have a high degree of a trait but may hardly have another trait even within the same domain. Just as unnaturally rigid diagnoses forced the creation of catch-all "not otherwise specified" diagnoses, the severity scales will likely put people into overly concrete subcategories that may harm diagnoses and interventions. The encouragement of more diagnoses may help people get more specific support for a wide range of challenges, but, like the expansion and addition of diagnoses, may lead to more overmedication or other problems. The *DSM-5* has not decided how to measure functional impairment, and even if it adopts an interactionist approach, how it will affect practice remains a mystery. The *DSM-5* has faced protests mainly because of concerns about overmedicalization, but if the medical profession could move away from a deficit focus to a more nuanced perspective like neurodiversity, it would address a substantial portion of the problem. Too often stigma and mistreatment results from not only from broader society, but also professional practices such as mental hospitals that could make anyone seem "ill" (Rosenhan, 1973).

Practical Implications

A historic window of opportunity has emerged to support more nuanced understandings of disability, with biomedical authorities increasingly admitting their shortcomings and disabled people strengthening our community. For example, this project, funded by the Autistic adult-oriented the Daniel Jordan Fiddle Foundation, represents a product of the larger neurodiversity movement instead of perpetuating a narrow focus on the autism spectrum. Biopsychosocial classifications that reflected the complex realities of disability threatened the psychiatric profession's authority, as it seemed to pathologize everyone (Wilson, 1993), so it invented an arbitrarily restrictive version of the medical model (Hyman, 2010). Now a more expansive system appears ready to return, causing concern among clinicians in addition to the public. We could welcome this trend if it comes with a comprehensive, valid, acceptable way to measure adaptive functioning, because ultimately everyone wants to improve people's quality of life (Anckarsäter, 2010), and if we counter the unrealistic, harmful deficit-only and normative focus.

Disabled college students with a "difference" rather than "deficit" view tend to feel better about their academics and have greater career ambitions, suggesting the need to raise awareness of neurodiversity (Griffin & Pollack, 2009). We can educate people, for example, about the difference between *disability* and *inability*. Ability can both mean potential, with acquired competencies known as *skills*, as well as current capacity or skill in an optimal setting, which may not match *performance* in everyday or demanding contexts for various reasons. Disabled people's challenges thus often reduce over time, especially when provided with needed environmental supports, which do not mean that we have heroically "overcome" our condition. Disabled people may simply do something differently (including using different parts of the brain for the same task), or take longer, or work harder (at least at first). With support we can enjoy quality of life, and sometimes we still can only do some aspects of a function or activity or do not do it as well (if at all), but society must critically consider whether that matters to us and what alternatives exist.

We also educate people to think of self-disclosure and self-advocacy as an *explanation,* not *excuse,* for need-based rights. Many people, including professionals, have stereotypes or use heuristics (shortcuts or rules of thumb) about disabilities. Simply disclosing a disability allows people to hold onto preconceptions about it, but educating them about how it affects you and tends to affect people in general may assist their understanding and your support. Sometimes people receive the support they need informally (not as a formal accommodation or service) through partial disclosure (describing specific needs but not revealing the condition) or other coping mechanisms, sometimes because of the costs or difficulties with obtaining a formal diagnosis (such as finding capable clinicians or uncertainty about how the condition manifests in adults). As more people receive diagnoses, self-understanding and support will increase overall, and the more people proactively advocate, stigma will likely reduce and people will become more comfortable with themselves.

Remember also that the diversity within and beyond disabilities creates uncertainty that leads even professionals to often misinterpret disabled people and order ineffective solutions, putting more responsibility on disabled people to own our disabilities and act as our strongest advocates. Under the Americans with Disabilities Amendments Act of 2008, "mitigating circumstances such" as learned behavior, medication, and assistive technology do not disqualify disabilities, so especially as adults our history and self-report may carry more weight than what outsiders can observe. Given scientists' search for truth and professionals' desire for authority, when confronted with insufficient evidence, they sometimes make up information. As the psychologist David Rosenhan said, "Whenever the ratio of what is known to what needs to be known approaches zero, we tend to invent knowledge and assume that we understand more than we actually do. We seem unable to acknowledge that we simply don't know" (1984, p. 139). Since, in such circumstances, professionals still often assume problems in the person rather than competence or problems in the environment, we have more reason to need to advocate for ourselves and take control over our lives.

References

Anckarsäter, H. (2010). Beyond categorical diagnostics in psychiatry: Scientific and medicolegal implications. *International Journal of Law and Psychiatry, 33,* 59-65.

Armstrong, T. (2010). Neurodiversity: Discovering the extraordinary gifts of autism, ADHD, dyslexia, and other brain differences. Cambridge, MA: Da Capo.

Astin, J.A., Shapiro, S.L., Eisenberg, D.M., & Forys, K.L. (2003). Mind-body medicine: State of the science, implication for practice. *Journal of the American Board of Family Medicine, 16,* 131-147.

Baker, D.L. (2011). *The politics of neurodiversity: Why public policy matters*. Boulder, CO: Lynne Rienner.

Beachamp-Pryor, K. (2011). Impairment, cure and identity: "Where do I fit in?" *Disability & Society, 26,* 5-17.

Borrell- Carrió, F., Suchman, A.L., & Epstein, R.M. (2004). The biopsychosocial model 25 years later: Principles, practice, and scientific inquiry. *Annals of Family Medicine, 2,* 576-582.Brickman, P., Rabinowitz, V.C., Karuza, J., Coates Jr., Cohn, D.E., & Kidder, L. (1982). Models of helping and coping. *American Psychologist, 37,* 368–384.

Bury, M. (2001). Illness narratives: Fact or fiction? *Sociology of Health & Illness, 23,* 263-285.

Charlton, J. (1998*). Nothing about us without us: Disability oppression and empowerment*. Berkeley: University of California Press.

Darling, R.B., & Heckert, D.A. (2010a). Activism, models, identities, and opportunities: a preliminary test of a typology of disability orientations. In Altman, B., & Barnatt, S. (Eds.), *Disability as a fluid state (Research in Social Science and Disability, 5)* (pp. 203–229).

Darling, R.B., & Heckert, D.A. (2010b). Orientations toward disability: Differences over the lifecourse. *Special Issue, Special Section: Measurement Issues in Ageing, Education, and Disability,* International *Journal of Disability, Development and Education, 57,* 131-143.

Donnellan, A.M. (1984). The criterion of the least dangerous assumption. *Behavior Disorders, 9,* 141-150.

Donnellan, A.M., Hill, D.A., & Leary, M.R. (2010). Rethinking autism: Implications of sensory and movement differences. *Disability Studies Quarterly, Special Issue: Autism and the Concept of Neurodiversity, 30*. Retrieved from http://www.dsq-sds.org/

Engel, G.L. (1977). The need for a new medical model: A challenge for biomedicine. *Science, 196,* 129-136.

Galvin, R.D. (2005). Researching the disabled identity: Contextualizing the identity transformation which accompany the onset of impairment. *Sociology of Health & Illness, 27,* 393-413.

Griffin, E., & Pollak, D. (2009). Student experiences of neurodiversity in higher education: Insights from the BRAINHE Project. *Dyslexia, 15,* 23-41.

Groopman, J., & Hartzband, P. (2011). *Your medical mind: How to decide what is right for you*. New York: Penguin.

Hahn, H. D., & Belt, T. L. (2004). Disability identity and attitudes toward cure in a sample of disabled activists. *Journal of Health and Social Behavior, 45,* 453-464.

Hyman, S.E. (2010). The diagnosis of mental disorders: The problem of reification. *Annual Review of*

Clinical Psychology, 6, 155-179.

Jamoom, E.W., Horner-Johnson, W., Suzuki, R., Andresen, E.M., Campbell, V.A., & the RRTC Expert Panel on Health Status Measurement. (2008). Age of disability onset and self-reported health status. *BMC Public Health, 8.* Retrieved online at http://www.biomedcentral.com/content/pdf/1471-2458-8-10.pdf.

King, G., Cathers, T., Brown, E., Specht, J.A., Willoughby, C., Polgar, J.M...Havens, L. (2003). Turning points and protective processes in the lives of people with chronic disabilities. *Qualitative Health Research, 13,* 184-205.

Lawton, J. (2003). Lay experiences of health and illness: Past research and future agendas. *Sociology of Health & Illness, 25,* 23-40.

Lechman, J.F., & March, J.S. (2011). Editorial: Developmental neuroscience comes of age. *Journal of Child Psychology and Psychiatry, 52,* 333-338.

Mayes, R. & Horwitz, A.V. DSM-III and the revolution in the classification of mental illness. *Journal of the History of the Behavioral Sciences, 2005,* 249-267.

McCarthy, H. (2003). The disability rights movement: Experiences and perspectives of selected leaders in the disability community. *Rehabilitation Counseling Bulletin, 46,* 209-223.

Petry , K., & Maes, B. (2009). Quality of life: People with profound intellectual and multiple disabilities. In J. Pawlyn & S. Carnably (Ed.), *Profound intellectual and multiple disabilities: Nursing complex needs* (pp. 15-36). Hoboken, NJ: Wiley-Blackwell.

Putnam, M. (2005). Conceptualizing disability: Developing a framework for political disability identity. *Journal of Disability Policy Studies, 16,* 188-198.

Rosenhan, D.L. (1984). On being sane in insane places. In P. Watzlawick (Ed.), *The invented reality: How do we know what we believe we know? Contributions to constructivism* (pp. 117-144). New York: Norton.

Rosenhan, D.L. (1973). On being sane in insane places. *Science, 179,* 250-258.

Rutter, M., Moffitt, T.E., & Caspi, A. (2006). Gene-environment interplay and psychopathology: Multiple varieties but real effects. *Journal of Child Psychology and Psychiatry, 47,* 226–261.

Shakespeare, T. (2008). Disability: Suffering, social oppression, or complex predicament? In M. Duwell et al. (eds.), *The contingent nature of life: Bioethics and the limits of human existence* (pp. 235–246). New York: Springer.

Shapiro, J. (1993). *No pity: People with disabilities forging a new civil rights movement.* New York: Times Books.

Swain, J., & French, S. (2000). Towards an affirmation model of disability. *Disability & Society, 15,* 569-582.

Weiner, B. (1993). On sin versus sickness: A theory of perceived responsibility and social motivation. *American Psychologist, 48,* 957-965.

Wilson, M. (1993). DSM-III and the transformation of American psychiatry: A history. *The American Journal of Psychiatry, 150,* 399-410.

Social Justice through Research

By Steven Kapp

Academic research, as an investment in the future, reflects the nature and prioritization of society's values. The topics, funding levels and sources (if anything), methodologies, outcomes, and framing of research all have ethical implications embedded in a sociocultural context. Research inherently takes a position on an eternally controversial topic, the meaning of knowledge itself and how people acquire or access it (a branch of philosophy known as *epistemology*). Indeed, *PhD*, the highest academic degree for most disciplines in the United States, stands for "Doctor of Philosophy". Therefore, understanding how people have constructed knowledge about disability may help you to conduct, assist, or influence disability research. This essay may help link you to ongoing, or influence new, research compatible with or actively promoting social justice, especially as concerns disabled people.

Academic philosophies and designs (Creswell, 2009)

Positivism underlies the scientific method and biomedical model. Originally and in a pure form, it assumes that absolute truth exists and that we can "positively" or definitely discover objective reality. As a *deterministic* philosophy, it believes that concrete causes control, rather than potentially contribute to, outcomes or effects. Moreover, as a *reductionist* philosophy, it tries to simplify complex phenomena to their most basic elements. It uses the *scientific method*, which believes that researchers must be able to test and verify *empirical* (observable) data to build evidence toward knowledge through *theories* (explanations) and *hypotheses* (predictions). Observable data can mean studying behavior, conducting experiments, or administering statistical instruments such as surveys or questionnaires. Thus, according to this worldview in theory and when applied to professional fields like medicine, disabilities inevitably worsen lives because of supposed deficits within their mind or body (often determined by unusual behavior), when researchers do not critically analyze observed differences between typical and disabled people.

For hundreds of years, many leading thinkers and scholars have recognized the shortcomings of a strict positivist philosophy, especially its claim that social matters can be studied as predictably and objectively as the physical world. Sometimes proponents (supporters) reflect this worldview with the revised name of *postpositivism*. This means that absolute truth does not exist or at least that people and research can never find it. Therefore, scientific evidence always has imperfections and rather than positively "proving" an idea, research can build evidence that supports, fails to reject, conflicts with, or even at least partially disproves – ideas. Scientists make claims and then revise or reject them depending on the body of evidence. Especially in the early development of a theory or claim, and especially if the research reflects stereotypes or potentially harmful ideas (in the case of disabilities, perhaps the argument that some people supposedly lack uniquely human abilities), it can be ethically questionable or dangerous for scientists to seek extensive public attention (such as in the media or popular books). With so much that remains unknown, and so many variables and possible exceptions, there is the risk that *conjectures*, or "educated guesses", can become assumed to be true, and lacking flexibility to the possibility of being wrong can and does pose real harm to people's lives.

(Post)positivists try to address this problem by continually aspiring for objectivity and avoiding or safeguarding against bias. As with absolute truth, this goal may seem noble but may be impossible to fully achieve or test. Academics refer to their lines of research as "interests", and their experiences, viewpoints, preferences, or desires somehow motivate or guide their work. How they frame the need for the study (introduction section of a paper), what questions they do or do not ask and predictions they make (aims and hypotheses), the procedures they choose to study them (methods), data analysis (results), and the interpretations they make of the results (discussion and sometimes conclusion). Daniel Sackett, M.D., in 1979 explained 56 biases of researchers that sometimes occur in clinical research. While the scientific method strives for *generalizability*, or the ability to accurately extend research findings to the entire population under study, even the recruitment of the *sample* of people to represent their group has flaws (for example, that some people are more willing or likely to participate in research than others; all too often researchers use a *convenience sample* of nearby college students, sometimes specific to their discipline, and assume they truly represent young adults or adults). Generally these problems have at least partial solutions, such as by having a large sample and the standard practice of a 99 percent *confidence interval* (reliability of a statistical estimate) in medical research and 95 percent confidence interval in most other social research, but even these can create more problems. Statistics and other forms of mathematics (and, similarly, theoretical computer science) constitute the *formal sciences* (formal systems of science; the results of studies are generally considered the scientific basis). While mathematical operations themselves are consistent and objective, how they are used are subject to many biases. (If you would like to learn more about biases, Wikipedia has articles on many types of statistical and cognitive biases: http://en.wikipedia.org/wiki/Bias.)

Despite its flaws, (post)positivism dominates disability research and among academic worldviews has the greatest influence on public policy and medical, clinical, educational, and various other settings that involve disabled people. The scientific method relies on numbers through *quantitative methods*, while *qualitative methods* analyze words and pictures through themes and patterns. However right or wrong, the research and often professional establishment tend to view quantitative research and (post)positivist principles as the most rigorous and "scientific" form of evidence. It forms the foundation of so-called *evidence-based medicine*, a trend over the last several decades where medical practices supposedly use the best available evidence. This idea in medicine has more recently moved to other fields, such as psychology and education. The "gold standard" of evidence at the group level is usually considered the *randomized controlled trial*, an experiment that randomizes participants to groups, at least one *experimental group,* where people experience the matter of interest (such as a therapy or an educational curriculum), and a *control group*, which tries to control for irrelevant variables. This design depends on averages and relatively large groups, possibly overlooking exceptions and other details. *Single-case experiments* (also known as *single-subject design*) are controlled studies in which participants serve as their own control and look for change over many periods (Chambless & Hollon, 1998).

Other worldviews and methods (qualitative methods and *mixed methods*, which combined qualitative and quantitative methods) have evolved relatively recently that seek to address the limitations of (post)positivism and the scientific method. They do not believe in absolute truth and generally acknowledge that people's values affect their research and sometimes actively base their research in them. This means that they embrace multiple truths or focus on the realities and goals that people construct about their own lives. While (post)positivism pre-determines study procedures with systematic rules and is traditional, other ways of doing research offer flexible alternatives that may emerge within the research process.

Here are some examples of qualitative and mixed methods. Qualitative strategies of inquiry include *ethnography*, which studies a cultural group in its natural setting over a long period of time. The researcher might have any combination of observation and participation regarding the group's activities, depending on the situation. *Case studies* examine someone or something in great depth, within a context. Although the medical model is associated with the scientific method, some doctors and psychologists have historically used it to study particular patients with a rare or little-known condition, or who have an unusual circumstance, often alongside other approaches. *Narrative research* involves people telling stories about their lives. *Grounded theory* refers to a technique of working from the bottom up to create a generalized theory, while other qualitative researchers prefer to work from the top down, such as by counting data and creating tree diagrams that organize them into categories (Erickson, 2004). Similarly, mixed methods approaches may combine qualitative and quantitative methods simultaneously, or use one to inform another, such as either using interviews to decide on a survey or after a survey following up with participants with interviews. They also may integrate the philosophies behind the methods.

These lines of research often focus on disadvantaged people and cultural minorities, who may feel misunderstood or marginalized by the establishment. They generally examine social or human problems in depth through understanding the subjective meanings individuals and groups assign to them. Yet the relatively open nature of this research sometimes gives researchers more power over the research process. Even studies devoted to giving voice to oppressed people's experiences may miss important meanings from the participants' perspectives if the researchers rely only on what the participants say, because what the people leave out may convey essential information (Charmaz, 2008). Therefore, while *(social) constructivism* refers to a philosophy in which meanings arise from a social context as people engage with the world, and thus tries to allow the themes of the research to emerge from the participants, researchers risk injecting their own perspective. The *participatory*, also known as *advocacy*, worldview avoids that problem by having researchers and members of the group under study collaborate on every stage of the research process. I work as a community member of the Academic Autism Spectrum Partnership in Research and Education, which describes the general research design among other matters on its web site (http://aaspire.org/). This philosophy generally has a political agenda of empowering minority groups and leading to change that improves their lives, and it is often associated with qualitative methods but can be used with quantitative or mixed methods. The *pragmatism* worldview focuses on practical problems and uses whatever other philosophies or methods are needed for what "works" at the time (e.g., Mcvilly, Stancliffe, Parmenter, & Burton-Smith, 2008).

Many quantitative researchers who subscribe to rigorous notions of science adopt pragmatic stances sometimes, such as referring to the organization of paper writing as "telling a story," which bridges a divide between numbers and narratives and raises further questions for the claim of absolute objectivity.

Orientation to these academic worldviews and research methods is influenced by the field of study. The *natural sciences* study the natural world (physics and other *physical sciences*, biology and other *life sciences*, Earth science, astronomy, and so on) and generally operate from a (post)positivist paradigm. Positivist philosophy assumes that the social world can be studied just like the natural world, especially for differences rooted in biology, a *basic science* to which positivist researchers have reduced disabled people. Yet people and society have great complexities, and research on them from the *behavioral* and *social sciences* do not always use the traditional scientific method, to try to better understand the different factors at play and the reasons for them. The behavioral and social sciences study people at an individual (like much of psychology), group (like social psychology), or societal (like sociology) level by their behavior and activities. The *humanities* include some social sciences but also applied fields like the visual and performing arts

Practical Implications for Doing Research

Different forms of research offer contrasting strengths and weaknesses, and you might consider how your options may help you to try to ultimately improve others' lives. The most powerful environments for disability are often, but not necessarily, relatively hostile to disabled activists. When applying to graduate schools, it struck me that many of the universities and fields that were more likely to openly espouse disability rights and justice were often relatively isolated and marginalized by more mainstream and influential counterparts. Disability studies, the humanities, and some social sciences are often relatively progressive, emphasize sociocultural aspects of disability and the human experience, and usually employ qualitative methods. Possibly there disabled activists might find relatively accessible mentorship, social support, and opportunities for advocacy. The fields that often have more direct impact on disabled people's lives, and the source of more controversy, include psychology, medicine (including psychiatry), and the biological sciences and are more conservative. They tend to use quantitative research and emphasize objectivity and the scientific method, as well as emphasize the limitations by the biological aspects of disability. The decision of what to study depends on what you want to learn, who you want your audience to be, and your career goals.

I decided to go to study in a fairly conservative field (psychology) at a leading, mainstream university (University of California, Los Angeles). I sometimes have felt somewhat isolated in my views or work and sometimes have to work harder to make my point than I might elsewhere. Nevertheless, I also appreciate the accommodations and attention I have received, and I bring a perspective that many people appreciate. I am learning more about what I like, what I think may benefit from some modifications, and what I think really needs to change. I try to bring relatively critical or progressive ideas into clinical settings, following the standards of my field to reach an influential audience. I publish in both traditional and critical outlets. I want to keep opportunities flexibly open for myself.

Remember that as a student and only one person you must honor your responsibilities to the groups and systems in which you participate, even as you might seek to improve some practices. When you choose to work as a team, you have limited freedom; the group's interests may conflict with your own on some matters. Researchers may have certain expectations or rules without explicitly articulating them, even though they may differ by field or research lab. Before making a final decision about whether or how to participate in an activity, you might respectfully ask or otherwise learn how much choice you have in the matter. If relevant, you might try to support your arguments by explaining and sharing relevant research evidence or ideas. You can also make suggestions about respectful language, but you may not have much control over matters like problematic funding organizations. If you have ethical or political objections to some aspect of the work but must choose between doing them or risking your working relationship or other potential growth opportunities, to decide if you will tolerate them you might consider how serious your objections are, how much they are definite or a matter of perspective, how you generally feel about the work now, and what benefits or costs it might have to offer your future. You might need to make some compromises to work with or under some people for particular projects or at a particular point in your career, but know that you would have other opportunities to be less constrained, such as by working with more philosophically aligned people for a different project, working by yourself, the activities you do outside of research, and the work you might do after you finish your education.

While you honor your responsibilities, as a student or researcher you can also exercise rights to try to help your academic community maintain professional standards of integrity. You have rights such as to keep your personal life private, including your disability (even if the people in your surroundings study it) where it has no relevance to your work, and to receive proper credit for your work. Many disciplines at least suggest as a guideline that the order of *authorship* (listing of the authors' names; *authors* substantially contribute to and get credit for, but do not necessarily write or sometimes even edit, papers) reflect the significance of contributions rather than considerations like seniority. Fields also have ethical codes of conduct for research and practice, and if you observe violations of them you have some rights such as telling a relevant authority if necessary. Academics as a profession strive for *collegiality* – collaborating in a friendly manner or sharing or critiquing ideas respectfully as a community – and any researcher should seek that ideal rather than selfish power or status.

Suggestions for Research

Understanding People with Disabilities

Disabled people need to be fully included in research about them, such as through participatory action research that combines scientific rigor with community needs. People with a variety of disabilities have expressed the need for this kind of research (Kitchin, 2000). This belief applies, of course, to people with intellectual disabilities (McDonald, Kidney, & Patka, 2012), who may require substantial support to participate, and the research process may positively challenge the views of nondisabled researchers toward disability and their profession (Bigby & Frawley, 2010).

Similarly, research should ask people with disabilities about their opinion on the objectives and priorities of research about them, from whether they want a cure to how to refer to them.

Respectful language must be used, and not disrespectful language such as claims that people are "afflicted with" a disability. For example, the writing style of the American Psychological Association (2010) says people with disabilities are only "patients" in the same contexts as nondisabled people, like vistiing a doctor. It also states, "Respect people's preferences; call people whtat they prefer to be called" (p. 72). This means that while it generally encourages the use of "people with disabilities," this use of language may be inappropriate for some people, such as those who identify with Deaf or Autistic culture.

You could support research that disproves the idea of a direct match between "severity" of disability and functioning. For example, some disabilities do not have clear effects on physical appearance and when subtler others may judge the other person as having a character flaw like selfish or lazy rather than requiring understanding and accommodation as a disabled person (Hinshaw & Stier, 2008).

Given how little we know about biology, we need to exert particular caution with biological studies and not assume that all differences in brains and genes indicate deficits. One way of addressing this problem is to include practical measures in such studies, such as connecting self-report to brain scans. For instance, a recent study showed the difference between cognitive and affective empathy (understanding and feeling the emotions of others, respectively) and their variation in nondisabled adults through the responses of their brain networks and in clinical questionnaires (Cox et al., in press).

You may wish to bring attention to significant challenges that are often neglected or misunderstood. Perhaps, for instance, you might think that a condition considered a mental disability has important physical aspects, including how the body senses or moves.

On the other hand, you may want to qualify or challenge deficit-based theories you find inaccurate and harmful, such as about disabled people's ability to understand themselves and express our own needs.

Moreover, you might study the strengths and positive experiences or contributions of people with disabilities.

You can study matters that reflect the lived experience of people with disabilities, many of which have relevance to clinical and medical researchers but are unlikely to be asked by them. This can often be done through interviews, especially when first gathering information, and can include topics like coping strategies people with disabilities develop over time. More importantly, it can ask people with disabilities to explain the functions their behaviors serve.

The diagnosis of stereotypic movement disorder describes repetitive body movements ("e.g., hand shaking or waving, body rocking, head banging, mouthing of objects, self-biting, hitting own body") as "seemingly driven and nonfunctional" (American Psychiatric Association, 2010). The description of "nonfunctional" is proposed to be changed to "apparently purposeless," which at least shows progress of indicating appearance to possibly misunderstanding outsiders. If the professionals asked people who engage in such behaviors, they might understand their purpose, and the possible danger in listing harmless behaviors like body rocking alongside harmful ones like head banging.

Studying the intersections of disability and other demographic characteristics, like age, gender, class, race, ethnicity, immigration status, and culture, can help to address challenges facing disadvantaged groups, such as being underserved or having less common attitudes toward social systems related to identifying and supporting disabilities.

Supporting People with Disabilities

The progressive values of the disability rights movement should be tested through research on services, including through academically conservative means. For example, quantitative research that used well-matched groups found that autistic adults and adults with intellectual disabilities earned more money and cost less to serve through supported employment rather than sheltered workshops, suggesting better vocational outcomes and economic savings for an inclusive rather than segregated setting (Cimera, 2011; Cimera, Wehman, West, & Burgess, 2012).

Similarly, research can merge progressive disability theory and activism with practical topics, including through traditional research methods. For instance, Goodrich and Ramsey (2012) used statistical questionnaires to evaluate disabled people's experiences with services. Disabled participants rated retailers lowest on accessibility, with social factors like assurance and empathy most related to perceptions of service quality. Disabled people who affirmed pride in their disability, as opposed to orientations like viewing it as a tragedy, placed higher value on the need for better accessibility and stronger service. Studies like this indicate the need for greater inclusiveness and respect for people with disabilities and that as demand for accommodations grows businesses can better compete by establishing themselves as "disability-friendly."

Without clear information that people desire recovery or cure, goals and measures should emphasize adaptive skills and quality of life rather than reduction of symptoms or normalization for its own sake. Many therapists working with autistic people, for example, have begun to evaluate effectiveness not by whether people lose their diagnosis, but rather by their functioning in daily activities (Tsatsanis, Saulnier, Sparrow, & Cicchetti, 2011).

You can assist with research testing self-advocacy programs designed to help people with disabilities lead decisions about their lives. Interventions may improve the social environment in addition to or as part of building people with disabilities' adaptive skills. For example, a recent study by Connie Kasari et al. (2012) found training typically developing peers at school to improve autistic children's social skills and inclusion more effective than traditional therapies directed one-on-one by an adult. (Reading Dr. Kasari's interpretation of the preliminary results helped me decide to study under her advisement. In particular, I liked that she said, "So maybe our best intervention is to intervene with the classroom as a whole, the teachers, the aides, the students. While [autistic] kids need some social skills intervention, if the environment isn't ready to receive them, it goes nowhere."

This contributed to a sense that I could find a place in the clinical, mainstream setting of educational psychology at the University of California, Los Angeles, where I could learn what I support in the field and what and how I would like to make changes.)

One classic treatment comparison to ask people with disabilities about is medication and talk therapy. Psychotherapy might seem more educational and less medical in that people actively learn skills through a technique individualized through a relationship, while drugs are taken more passively in a more prepackaged way and directly affect the brain. Yet critics of medication or pharmaceutical companies might be surprised that many people with disabilities are quite grateful. Medication is often more convenient and less demanding, variable, and expensive than psychotherapy and may be at least as effective with no more side effects for many people. People with disabilities may often say that medication and psychotherapy work well together.

The effect of lifestyle, such as physical exercise, sleep, and diet, likely helps with health promotion in a way that supports daily living with disabilities. This might include traditional approaches as well as "alternative" ones such as yoga and dietary supplements. The degree of help and whether it could reduce or eliminate the need for some forms of more formal support could benefit from more research.

Social and Systems Change on Campus
By Steven Kapp

Many contributors to this handbook have written excellent chapters related to social or systems change in higher education, often with personal examples such as leading student organizations. This essay organizes that theme by beginning with broad suggestions illustrated by my own experiences, in chronological order from beginnings in high school to more extensive efforts as an undergraduate and now in graduate school. Diagnosed with Asperger's at about age 13, I did not become aware of the disability rights movement and disability culture until about my sophomore year as an undergraduate, around the time I switched to a major in public policy and added a minor in professional communication. As I began to become more engaged with organizations, conferences, and papers related to the autism spectrum and disabilities more widely, I moved on to a PhD program in educational psychology to study related issues. That more recent focus helped to inform my essays for this handbook on disability models and research.

Begin with a realistic goal, working step by step

In high school and my first three semesters at college, my greatest effort to change relations on campus involved the issue of peace between Jews and Muslims. I offer it as an example because if I had learned from the differences between my success in high school and disappointment in college, I might have accomplished more with my early ambitions of strengthening the disability community in college.

I strengthened the relationships between the Jewish and Muslim student clubs in high school. While I was a sophomore and my sister was a senior and co-president of the Jewish club, it with the Muslim club created a peace T-shirt. I was not involved at the time and did not know how they achieved this feat, but it motivated me, as president of the Jewish club in my own senior year, to continue the alliance. I initiated discussions into two collaborative events, one in which we both brought a leader of our faith to speak to the other club to share and educate, and another where we shared a booth at our school's club fair. I presented my idea to have a peace T-shirt that included an acrostic poem:

Peace
Evolves
As a
Common
Endeavor

Students expressed some interest but did not see it as a high priority, in part because we had already done this two years ago.

In college (at the University of Southern California) I had an ambitious plan to create a peace T-shirt involving the 10 Jewish, Muslim, Israeli, and Palestinian religious, political, and residential groups on campus. I joined one of the Jewish organizations but was not familiar with most of the other organizations, so I learned as I went along. I shared the proposed design (the names of the organizations forming the outline of a dove on one side and the short poem on the other) and secured a $300 pledge from the university's religious life office. Each organization supported the idea at some point, with eight in support at one point. Nevertheless, it collapsed because of the demands of more traditional religious groups, political groups that were committed to opposing goals, and residential groups that had to live together. If I had begun with a more modest plan involving a moderate pair of Jewish and Muslim student organizations, it likely would have worked, as it did in high school. As it happened, tensions emerged that reflected those by believers beyond the safer and more open confines of a diverse university, and without having laid a foundation of working relationships or collaborative events, my goal seemed immature. The shirt would be a symbol, and without concrete progress for it to represent, its message may have seemed hollow to people who might have grown more suspicious of one another. Meanwhile, the challenge risked harming my academics, as I did not allow myself much time to adjust to the transition to college and sometimes suspended my efforts when I feared my grades would slip.

In the spring semester of my sophomore year, Scott Robertson of the Autistic Self Advocacy Network (ASAN) contacted me and introduced me to the neurodiversity and disability rights movements. Now I had a growing desire to change the university in this direction. Other minority groups had assemblies (appointed by the student government) programming activities for them, but not disabled students. I talked with the president of the board in charge of student programming, who it turns out happened to also be disabled, and got her support for the idea for working toward a disability assembly. I met with the director of the student disability office and received his support as well. Yet all assemblies needed to consist of student organizations, but there were no student-serving disability-related organizations with a scope beyond fundraising on campus (let alone a Disability Awareness or Disability Pride Week). So this time the system required me to work at a more basic grassroots level in order to change it. (On the previous topic I met with the leaders of organizations, often without having met people in lower or unranked positions).

Ally with committed people you can trust

I turned my attention to creating a disability student organization, but did not have much help. I met a nondisabled student who started a Facebook group for autism awareness for our university (her autistic cousin led to her interest in autism). I could see immediately that she was also politically minded (studying political science, in addition to the messages she wrote on Facebook). I had less awareness of what forms problematic "awareness" and fundraising campaigns could take, so I did not fully see the signs of how her beliefs differed from mine and thought I could work with her on an area with less relevance to the more controversial issues. We planned to start a student disability organization together, but it turned out she never was organized or committed enough, despite my repeated attempts to work with her.

In the fall of my junior year she ran for vice president of the student government, pledging to create a student disability coalition. The campaign manager of the main opponent ticket was an autistic friend of mine, who also had pledged to start a student organization with me but this never happened. That campaign pledged to increase the number of disabled people in student government, which my friend thought was more realistic and actionable. Perhaps he was right about his disability proposal, and maybe also other arguments for voting for his ticket, but my hopes that plans with the other student would work out may have hurt my judgment. The vice presidential candidate lost and was too busy or unmotivated to help me with my own efforts beyond the paperwork to register the organization.

After my previous appointments, I may have felt desperate for help and did not exercise the judgment and patience I needed to finding people worthy of my trust and partnership. Group members and allies need to be willing and able to work with you, with a compatible agenda.

Do not personally take on too much work

In the spring of my junior year, I started a student disability organization with little help but did not receive help beyond that a casual friend from another organization assisted with a flyer. I needed a list of a few students to get the organization registered, but none of them were committed to the organization. I named it Alliance of Students with Disabilities (same initials as "autism spectrum disorder"; I had thought about creating an autism-specific group at some point but decided to start broader). I worked hard to conceptualize, plan, organize, and recruit for the one meeting it had. I created a panel about autism with four people; five other students (including my autistic friend but not the other political student) showed up. I thought it was a beneficial event for those who attended. I made a friend from the panel, but I do not think the outcome was worth my effort. Again, I risked harming my grades and other balance in my life, and my attempts increased my already high stress.

Try not to give up hope or miss out on new opportunities

By the fall of my senior year, I was not actively looking to create a larger disability presence on campus, but tried again when an opportunity emerged before me. My hopes had waned on what I could do, given disappointments and a shrinking time window before graduation. Meanwhile, I was more focused on graduate school applications, which were related to studying disability, and knew that I would be dedicating my career to the rights and welfare of disabled people. I was heavily involved on campus, including related to disabilities (for example, I served as an officer for the local chapter of Best Buddies, which also paired me with other developmentally disabled students), and my classes were more demanding. Then I saw a candidate running for, coincidentally, vice president of student government in my dining hall; I brought up my concerns about disability issues on campus with her. This led to a meeting with a student in the government, and she organized and had sponsored the event I suggested: wheelchair basketball, bringing in local disabled competitive athletes to play with interested students. She also was committed to my goal of a Disability Awareness Week, and the first annual one began the following year. Progress may come more effectively and efficiently from strategically making connections than from working hard in the sense of expending a lot of energy.

Consider reaching out to the organized disability, and the broader, communities

I have been more successful with co-directing a chapter of ASAN in graduate school (at the University of California, Los Angeles), than I was starting a new organization as an undergraduate student. Part of the reason is that, like the help from the student government, a preexisting, established organization may have stronger resources, but you should make sure that the organization matches your beliefs and goals. In addition to the greater balance through sharing responsibility with a co-director (Sarah Pripas), this chapter has been more sustainable than my own organization in part because it is open to people from the local area who are not part of the university (who can find out about the group from a blog, Facebook, and Meetup.com). As I did before, we try to recruit and have in our audience both disabled and nondisabled people.

Education or raising positive awareness can be an effective strategy and influence people in the field

The professional fields where attitudes and practices have traditionally caused the most resistance from disability activists are medical and clinical, such as medicine and psychology. UCLA has some of the leading programs and research centers in these areas regarding autism and other disabilities, from a mainstream perspective that is often disconnected from disability culture or empowerment. Shortly after my graduate studies began, my ASAN chapter had a Neurodiversity 101 event with six panelists and about 35 attendees, many of whom were medical or clinical researchers, practitioners, or advocates. Many of these professionals may not have been aware of the civil rights-oriented neurodiversity movement of various neurological disabilities, and we received good feedback from them.

Systems change may require powerful alliances

Changing the ways systems serve disabled people often involves working with relevant structures, programs, or offices, sometimes building friendly relations with organizations that do constructive work and have influential people interested in collaborating to possibly change other organizations or systems. UCLA has a University Committee on Disability, University Center of Excellence on Developmental Disabilities (UCEDD), Disability Awareness Week, disability studies program, and in my experience more accommodating student disability office than USC. Even within an institution with some elements of concern, you might find others that proactively support you. The director of the UCEDD is a progressive ally who helped us plan and reserve room for the neurodiversity panel and served on it. She has invited Sarah and me to the UCEDD's Advisory Committee meetings; recently I have helped to draft the UCEDD's 5-year plan.

I hope to address systemic issues that might interest you too, such as unidentified and unregistered disabled students and improving accommodations and services on campus (many colleges do not have adequate funding or therapists for the student counseling center and deny many students help or refer them out, for example). Especially for colleges that do ethically questionable disability research, you might see if they will add disabled people (whether specific to a disability or more broadly) to an advisory committee or a hold a public forum on ethical issues in disability research. Remember also to consider engaging in advocacy outside of campus that affects issues on and beyond it, such as at conferences and through legislative advocacy – perhaps on a task force or committee for the state or a policy summit for the state or country. Those activities may help you to understand the nature and status of broader issues and reach a greater array of stakeholders, helping you put in context your journey as a leader in college and beyond.

Notes

Notes

Notes

Notes

Notes

Notes